Quick Reference

to

Renal
CRITICAL CARE
NURSING

Aspen Series
Quick Reference to Critical Care Nursing
Joan M. Vitello-Cicciu, RN, CCRN, CS, Series Editor
Clinical Care Nurse Specialist, Surgical Critical Care
The University Hospital at Boston University Medical Center
Boston, Massachusetts

Editor
The Journal of Cardiovascular Nursing
Aspen Publishers, Inc.
Gaithersburg, Maryland

Quick Reference to Neurological Critical Care Nursing
Noreen M. Leahy

Quick Reference to Respiratory Critical Care Nursing
Nancy L. Kranzley

Quick Reference to Dysrhythmia Identification and Intervention
Molly A. Johantgen

Quick Reference to Cardiac Critical Care Nursing
Janet S. Eagan
Susan L. Stewart
Joan M. Vitello-Cicciu

Quick Reference

to

Renal
CRITICAL CARE
NURSING

Janice Weems, RN, MSN
Shift Manager
Maternity Pavilion
Former Clinical Nurse Specialist
Transplant Unit
University of Alabama Hospital

Aspen Series
Quick Reference to Critical Care Nursing
Joan M. Vitello-Cicciu, Series Editor

AN ASPEN PUBLICATION®
Aspen Publishers, Inc.
Gaithersburg, Maryland
1991

Library of Congress Cataloging-in-Publication Data

Weems, Janice.
Quick reference to renal critical care nursing / Janice Weems.
p. cm. (Aspen series quick reference to critical care nursing)
Includes bibliographical references and index.
ISBN: 0-8342-0248-4
1. Kidneys Diseases Nursing Handbooks, manuals, etc.
2. Intensive care nursing Handbooks, manuals, etc. I. title. II. Series.
[DNLM: 1. Critical Care handbooks. 2. Kidney Failure, Acute nursing
handbooks. 3. Kidney Failure, Chronic nursing handbooks. WY 39
W397q]
RC903.W44 1991
616.6 1 dc20
DNLM/DLC
for Library of Congress
91-18033
CIP

Aspen Publishers, Inc., grants permission for photocopying for limited personal
or internal use. This consent does not extend to other kinds of copying, such
as copying for general distribution, for advertising or promotional purposes,
for creating new collective works, or for resale. For information, address
Aspen Publishers, Inc., Permissions Department, 200 Orchard Ridge Drive,
Gaithersburg, Maryland 20878.

The authors have made every effort to ensure the accuracy of the information
herein, particularly with regard to drug selection and dose. However, appropriate
information sources should be consulted, especially for new or unfamiliar drugs or
procedures. It is the responsibility of every practitioner to evaluate the appropriateness of a particular opinion in the context of actual clinical situations and with due
consideration to new developments. Authors, editors, and the publisher cannot be
held responsible for any typographical or other errors found in this book.

Editorial Services: Barbara Marsh

Library of Congress Catalog Card Number: 91-18033
ISBN: 0-8342-0248-4

Printed in the United States of America

1 2 3 4 5

This book is dedicated to my sister, Sandra,
who constantly encouraged me.

Table of Contents

Foreword

Today, as an evolution of sub-specialization, many types of critical care units exist, which mandate that nurses keep abreast of constantly changing technology and the application of new knowledge. One such area of subspecialization is renal critical care nursing. This *Quick Reference to Renal Critical Care Nursing* textbook addresses the spectrum of renal disease. The author of this book has taken her vast clinical experience with these subsets of patients and has translated it into this quick reference format for easy and rapid access to information.

Ms. Weems addresses the acute, as well as chronic, problems plaguing the renal patient. She expertly intertwines the medical with the nursing aspects of patient care. I envision this text as a needed reference for not only critical care nurses, but also medical-surgical nurses and students caring for patients with renal disease.

The author is to be commended for writing such a clinically relevant text. This book is a superb compendium to the Quick Reference Critical Care Nursing Series.

Joan M. Vitello-Cicciu, RN, MSN,
    CCRN, CS
Clinical Nurse Specialist
Surgical Critical Care
The University Hospital at Boston
    University Medical Center
Boston, Massachusetts

Preface

Today's critical care nurse is faced with many challenges, including that of caring for patients with renal disease or complications. In order to provide comprehensive health care to these patients, critical care nurses need precise knowledge of the physiological and psychological impact of renal disease.

Quick Reference to Renal Critical Care Nursing reviews renal anatomy, physiology, diseases, dialysis, and transplantation and in doing so provides a strong foundation for an improved understanding of these patients. Both practicing nurses and nursing students will benefit from this book's comprehensive content and concise outline format, which facilitates rapid and selective retrieval.

This book reflects my desire to offer my own clinical experience to fellow clinicians and to help them improve the quality of life of those who face renal problems and disease.

1
Anatomy

THE KIDNEYS

Location

The kidneys lie to the right and the left of the lumbar spine (between the 12th thoracic and 3rd lumbar vertebrae) on the posterior wall of the abdominal cavity, in the retroperitoneal space (Figure 1-1). The right kidney is lower than the left kidney because of the location of the liver. The kidneys move downward during inspiration, as the diaphragm contracts.

The kidneys are covered by a tough capsule surrounded by a cushion of fat, supported by fasciae. The kidneys anteriorly are protected by abdominal muscles, fasciae, fat, and the intestines; posteriorly, by back muscles and ribs.

Size

Each kidney is approximately 5 to 7 cm wide, 11 to 13 cm long, and 2.5 cm thick. Each adult kidney weighs approximately 120 to 160 g.

Gross Structure

Hilus

The hilus is the indentation on the side of the kidney where the renal artery, renal vein, lymphatics, nerves, and ureters enter the kidney (Figure 1-2).

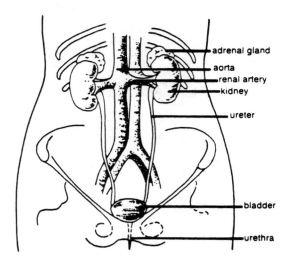

Figure 1-1 Gross anatomy of the renal system. *Source:* From *Core Curriculum for Nephrology Nursing* (p. 31) by L.E. Lancaster, 1987, Pitman, NJ: American Nephrology Nurses' Association. Copyright 1987 by American Nephrology Nurses' Association. Reprinted by permission.

Cortex

The cortex is the outer portion of the kidney; it contains 85% of the nephrons (cortical nephrons) and their blood vessels. The cortex also contains the glomerulus, Bowman's capsule, and the proximal and distal tubules of the juxtamedullary nephrons, which are located deep in the cortex.

Medulla

The medulla is the inner portion of the kidney that contains the pyramids, renal columns (Bertin's columns), loops of Henle, vasa recta, and collecting ducts of the juxtamedullary nephrons.

Pyramids. The pyramids are located in the medulla and are triangular structures composed of nephrons and their blood vessels (Figure 1-3).

Renal Columns. Renal columns are cortical tissue between the pyramids.

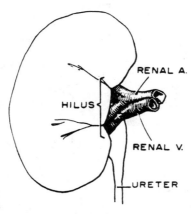

Figure 1-2 Gross structure of the kidney. *Source:* Reproduced by permission from S.A. Anderson and L.M. Wilson, *Pathophysiology,* 3rd ed., 1986, New York: McGraw-Hill. Copyright 1986 by The C.V. Mosby Company, St. Louis

Microscopic Structure

The functional unit of the kidney is the nephron. Each kidney contains approximately 1 million nephrons; 85% are located in the cortex (cortical nephrons) and 15% are located in the medulla (juxtamedullary nephrons) (Figure 1-4).

Glomerulus

The glomerulus is a collection of capillaries. It arises directly from the afferent arteriole and is positioned in Bowman's capsule. The glomerular membrane has a large surface area and is semipermeable to allow the passage of fluid and solute. Three cell layers of the glomerular membrane enhance its permeability.

1. The innermost layer is composed of endothelial cells that are porous and promote easy movement of water and solute.
2. The middle layer, or basement membrane, is less porous.
3. The outer layer is composed of epithelial cells. The sizes of the pores of the middle and outer layers affect the passage of large molecules.

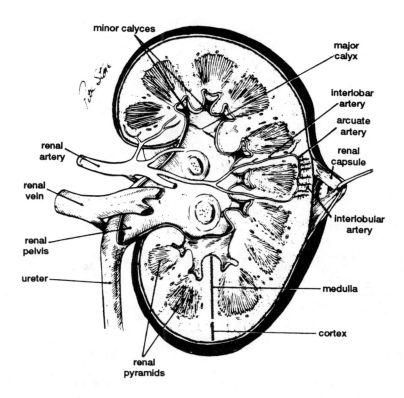

Figure 1-3 A longitudinal section of the kidney, showing the pyramids and other structures. *Source:* Reproduced by permission from L.L. Langley, I. Telford, and J. Christensen, *Dynamic Anatomy and Physiology*, 5th ed., 1980, New York: McGraw-Hill. Copyright 1980 by The C.V. Mosby Company, St. Louis.

Tubules

The tubules extend beyond Bowman's capsule and are composed of four segments, each of which has a different structure and function.

1. The proximal convoluted tubule arises from the glomerulus and is primarily responsible for reabsorption.
2. The loop of Henle begins in the renal medulla and is a U-shaped structure with two different parts: a descending loop and an ascending loop. The primary function of the loop of Henle is to concentrate urine.

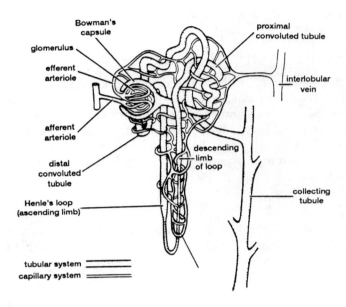

Figure 1-4 Components of the nephron. *Source:* Reproduced by permission from M.W. Gröer and M.E. Shekelton, *Basic Pathophysiology*, 3rd ed., St. Louis, 1989, © The C.V. Mosby Company.

3. The distal convoluted tubule forms after the ascending loop of Henle. Its primary functions are reabsorption of sodium and water and secretion of hydrogen and potassium.
4. The collecting duct forms as the terminal portion at the juncture of two or more distal tubules. The collecting duct then passes through the medulla, where it joins other ducts to create a papillary duct. The papillary duct empties into the minor calix and then into the remaining urinary collecting system.

Blood Supply

Blood Flow

Renal blood flow is approximately 1200 mL/min, or 20% to 25% of the cardiac output. Approximately 90% of the renal blood supply circulates through the cortex at a rate of 4.5 mL/min, and 10% circulates through the medulla at a rate of 1 mL/min.

Afferent Arterioles

A single renal artery supplies blood to each kidney. The renal artery branches off the abdominal aorta and enters the kidney at the hilus. At the hilus, it divides into two branches that travel toward the dorsal and ventral regions of the kidney and form interlobar arteries. At the point of the corticomedullary junction they become arcuate arteries. Arcuate arteries form multiple afferent arterioles and supply the glomerulus of the nephron (Figure 1-5).

Efferent Arterioles

Glomeruli are drained by efferent arterioles. Efferent arterioles empty the cortical nephrons and branch off into a capillary network that supplies blood to other tubules in that area.

Vasa Recta

In the juxtamedullary glomeruli, efferent arterioles flow into the vasa recta. The vasa recta supply the tubules in the medulla. Capillaries in the

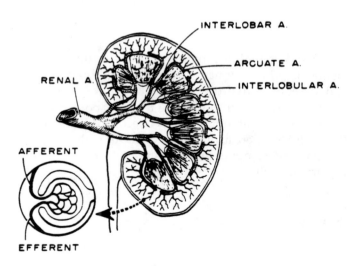

Figure 1-5 Longitudinal section of the kidney showing renal vasculature. *Source:* Reproduced by permission from S.A. Price and L.M. Wilson, *Pathophysiology*, 3rd ed., 1986, New York: McGraw-Hill. Copyright 1986 by the C.V. Mosby Company, St. Louis.

outer cortex eventually drain into interlobar veins and arcuate veins (Figure 1-6).

Nerve Innervation

The kidneys are innervated by the sympathetic branches from the celiac plexus; upper lumbar, splanchnic, and thoracic nerves; and intermesenteric and superior hypogastric plexuses, which join to form a surrounding renal plexus.

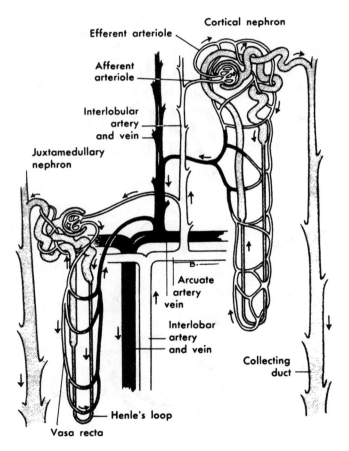

Figure 1-6 Blood supply of nephron. *Source:* From *Nursing Management of Renal Problems*, 2nd ed., by D.J. Brundage, 1980, St. Louis: C.V. Mosby Co. Copyright 1980 by the author. Reprinted by permission.

THE URINARY TRACT

Urine passes from the renal pelvis via the ureters to the urinary bladder. The urinary bladder releases urine through the urethra (Figure 1-7).

Ureters

Ureters are mucosa-lined fibromuscular tubes that transport urine by peristalsis from the renal pelvis to the bladder. Ureters are approximately 30 to 33 cm long and 2 to 8 cm in diameter.

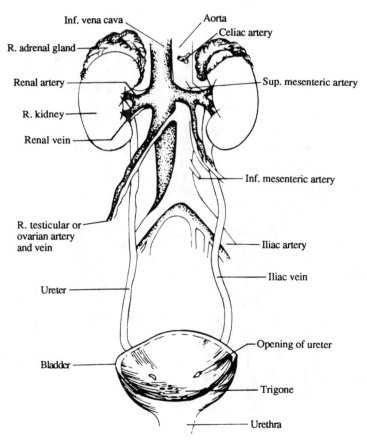

Figure 1-7 Anatomical location of the kidneys in relation to other organs. *Source:* From *Renal Problems in Critical Care* (p. 4) by L. Schoengrund and P. Balzer (Eds.), 1985, New York: John Wiley and Sons, Inc. Copyright 1985 by Delmar Publishers, Inc. Reprinted by permission.

Urinary Bladder

The urinary bladder is a muscular sac located in the anterior pelvis and inferior to the peritoneal cavity, posterior to the pubic bones. The normal capacity of the bladder of an adult is 300 to 500 mL. The orifices from the ureters and the urethra comprise the trigone.

Urethra

The urethra is a tube that transports urine from the bladder to the urinary meatus for excretion. The urethra of a man is approximately 20 cm long; the urethra of a woman is 3 to 5 cm long.

SUGGESTED READINGS

Guyton, A.C. (1986). *Textbook of medical physiology* (7th ed.). Philadelphia: Saunders.

Hekelman, F. P., & Ostendarp, C. A. (1979). *Nephrology nursing perspectives of care.* New York: McGraw-Hill.

Lancaster, L.E. (1987). Anatomy and physiology of the renal system. In L.E. Lancaster (Ed.), *Core curriculum for nephrology nursing.* Pitman, NJ: American Nephrology Nurses' Association.

Schoengrund, L., & Balzer, P. (Eds.). (1985). *Renal problems in critical care.* New York: Wiley.

Stark, J.L. (1988). Renal anatomy and physiology. In M.R. Kinney, D.R. Packa, & S.B. Dunbar (Eds.), *AACN's clinical reference for critical care nursing* (2nd ed.). New York: McGraw-Hill.

2
Physiology

INTRODUCTION

The kidney contributes to homeostasis by regulation of water and electrolyte balance, regulation of acid-base balance, and excretion of waste products. Metabolically, the kidney regulates blood pressure through the secretion of renin, and activates vitamin D_3. The kidney also secretes the hormone erythropoietin.

WATER BALANCE

Water balance is achieved by the thirst-neurohypophysial-renal mechanism, which guarantees that intake equals output. The water regulatory mechanism basically functions by stimulating the thirst mechanism to promote water intake and by adjusting urine volume according to the presence or absence of antidiuretic hormone and renal regulation (Figure 2-1).

Antidiuretic Hormone

Antidiuretic hormone (ADH) is synthesized in the ventromedian nucleus of the hypothalamus by specialized nerve cells. After it is formed, ADH moves down the supraoptic tracts, where it is stored in the posterior pituitary gland. After its release from the posterior pituitary gland, ADH moves to the distal tubule and collecting duct of the nephron. The tubular cells in these two areas of the nephron become highly permeable to water in the presence of ADH.

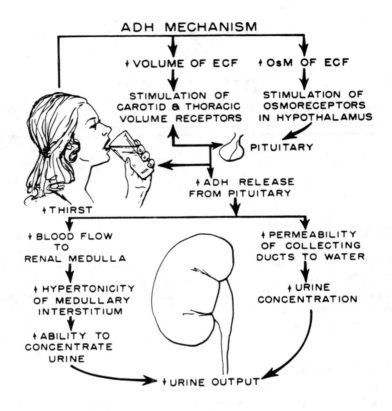

Figure 2-1 Mechanism of antidiuretic hormone (ADH). ECF, Extracellular fluid. *Source:* Reproduced by permission from S.A. Price and L.M. Wilson, *Pathophysiology,* 3rd ed., 1986, New York: McGraw-Hill. Copyright 1986 by The C.V. Mosby Company, St. Louis.

An increase in plasma osmolality is the primary stimulus for ADH release and interaction with the thirst mechanism. A change in extracellular fluid osmolality of only 1% to 2% initiates a reaction. Osmoreceptor cells in the hypothalamus perceive changes in plasma osmolality.

Osmoreceptors are specialized neurons located in or near the supraoptic nuclei of the anterior hypothalamus. These specialized neurons contain chambers filled with fluid and emit nerve impulses continuously. The fluid chambers respond specifically to changes in the concentration of extracellular fluid. The most effective stimulant is sodium. When the osmolality of the extracellular fluid decreases, water enters the fluid chambers in an attempt to establish equilibrium between the two fluids. This influx of water forces the fluid chambers to swell, resulting in a decreased rate of impulse discharge. Thus, fewer impulses are transmitted from the osmoreceptors to the supraoptic nuclei through the pituitary stalk to the neurohypophysis to promote the release of ADH, and less ADH is excreted.

An increase in the osmolality of extracellular fluid reverses the process. An increase in osmolality creates extracellular fluid that is hypertonic to the fluid in the chambers. Water leaves the fluid chambers and flows into the extracellular fluid, shifting the system toward equilibrium. This outflow of water results in a shrinking of the fluid chambers and an increase in the rate of impulse discharge to the neurohypophysis. The net effect is an increase in the secretion of ADH.

Normal plasma osmolality is 280 to 295 mOsm/L. Serum osmolality less than 280 mOsm/L represses the thirst mechanism and ADH. The kidney responds by excreting an extremely dilute urine. If the serum osmolality is greater than 280 mOsm/L, ADH is released up to the maximum of 295 mOsm/L. The kidney responds by producing a very concentrated urine through the absorption of solute-free water. The thirst mechanism is also stimulated and, in combination with the kidney's response, attempts to restore normal osmolality.

Another mechanism responsible for ADH release involves stretch receptors located in the carotid bodies and the aorta. These receptors are sensitive to changes in circulating blood volume or blood pressure. A decrease in blood volume of 7% to 15%, along with an increase in osmolality, is thought to stimulate ADH (Fairchild, 1980). Other factors that stimulate release of ADH are hypoxia, pain, and stress.

Countercurrent Mechanism and Glomerular-Tubular Balance

The kidney controls water balance by two means, the countercurrent mechanism and glomerular-tubular balance.

Countercurrent Mechanism

The countercurrent mechanism is the renal mechanism that controls normal urine dilution and concentration (Figure 2-2). Filtrate enters the loop of Henle after leaving the proximal tubule. The loop has two segments, a descending portion and an ascending portion, each with separate functions in altering the filtrate. The descending loop (the thin limb) is permeable only to water, while the ascending portion (the thick limb) has an active sodium chloride pump and is impermeable to water. The working combination of the two segments determines the concentration (osmo-

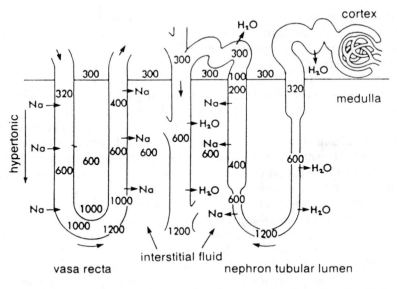

Figure 2-2 Countercurrent multiplying and exchange. *Source:* From *Core Curriculum for Nephrology Nursing* (p. 36) by L.E. Lancaster, 1987, Pitman, NJ: American Nephrology Nurses' Association. Copyright 1987 by American Nephrology Nurses' Association. Reprinted by permission.

lality) of urine. Urine osmolality can be adjusted within a wide range, from 50 to 1200 mOsm/L.

The loop of Henle also maintains the hyperosmolar concentration in the renal medulla. The countercurrent mechanism determines urine concentration and maintains a hypertonic renal interstitium. This mechanism is functional because of the anatomic positioning of the long descending and ascending loops of Henle in relation to the peritubular capillaries of the vasa recta. The loops act as concurrent multipliers; the capillaries act as concurrent exchangers. An isotonic glomerular filtrate of 300 mOsm/L leaves the proximal tubule and enters the descending loop of Henle. Water is gradually drawn into a hypertonic medullary interstitium because this loop is permeable only to water. The loss of water from the filtrate causes an increase in the osmolality. At the hairpin turn of the loop, the filtrate osmolality is dramatically increased, contributing concurrently to the formation of a hypotonic medullary interstitium.

A portion of the sodium chloride is lost as the filtrate progresses to the ascending limb of the loop of Henle. The medullary interstitium becomes more hypertonic again as its sodium concentration is increased by the pumping action at the ascending limb (Stark, 1985).

A dilute filtrate reaches the distal tubule. In the distal tubule, the filtrate is altered by the presence or absence of ADH. The presence of ADH results in the formation of concentrated urine; the absence of ADH produces the opposite effect, as dilute filtrate is excreted unchanged, creating a dilute urine with water excretion in excess of solute.

Glomerular-Tubular Balance

Glomerular-tubular balance is the mechanism by which the amount of fluid the tubules receive via glomerular filtration is related to the amount of fluid reabsorbed or excreted by the tubules. Hypovolemia or hypotension causes a decrease in glomerular blood flow, leading to a decrease in glomerular filtration rate (GFR). The tubules respond to a decreased filtration volume by reabsorbing salt and water, which decreases urine output. With an increase in GFR (e.g., expanded volume) the opposite effect takes place. The tubules respond to the increased flow rate by permitting the production and output of large volumes of urine. Both responses are attempts to restore fluid status to normal or to compensate for the altered fluid balance.

ELECTROLYTE BALANCE

The kidney filters large volumes of electrolytes daily, excreting only a very small amount into the urine. The kidney attempts to maintain an electrolyte balance by adjusting excretion of electrolytes.

The kidney plays a major role in sodium regulation. Physiologic determinants of renal sodium regulation include renal perfusion, aldosterone levels, and a suspected natriuretic factor, or third factor. Iatrogenic or pathophysiologic influences such as diuretics, nonreabsorbable anions in the filtrate, and intrinsic renal abnormalities also determine the balance between sodium intake and excretion.

Decreased renal perfusion and an elevated aldosterone level support increased sodium reabsorption and excretion. Diminished renal perfusion decreases GFR and, as a result, three factors support increased sodium reabsorption.

1. A lowered rate of flow through the tubules allows for more complete reabsorption of sodium by the active mechanism of the renal epithelial cells.
2. Decreased renal blood flow results in an increased filtration fraction. Since a greater than normal fraction of the plasma perfusing

the kidneys is filtered, the protein concentration of plasma leaving the glomerular capillaries and entering the postglomerular peritubular plasma increases the attraction for water from tubular to peritubular fluid. Increased water reabsorption contributes to increasing tubular sodium concentration and the concentration gradient promoting its recovery.

3. Decreased renal perfusion stimulates renin release from the juxtaglomerular cells of the afferent arteriole. Through the renin-angiotensin system, aldosterone secretion increases.

A natriuretic factor has yet to be isolated, but this factor is invoked to explain the observation that increased plasma volume and, hence, renal perfusion stimulate sodium excretion, regardless of plasma sodium concentration. It is believed that the natriuretic factor serves to maintain plasma volume rather than plasma osmolality.

The kidney is the primary regulator of potassium balance in the body, with the exception of a small amount of dietary potassium lost in the stool. Through its regulatory role, the kidney has an ability to adjust the body to wide variations in the quantity of dietary potassium. Dietary ingestion of a large quantity of potassium (500 mEq/day) can be followed by excretion of as much as 10 times that amount. Conservation of potassium is also possible, but it is not as effective as conservation of sodium.

Potassium excretion is influenced by a number of factors, including dietary intake, high tubular flow state, aldosterone, renal sodium load, acid-base balance, and renal ammonia production. In addition, there is a diurnal pattern of potassium excretion, which peaks at noon.

URINE FORMATION

The kidney also regulates fluid and electrolyte balance through urine formation in association with hormones such as ADH and aldosterone. Reabsorption, secretion, and excretion of water and solutes are involved in the process of urine formation through glomerular filtration, tubular reabsorption, and tubular secretion.

Glomerular Filtration

The first step in urine formation is glomerular filtration. It begins as blood enters the glomerulus via the afferent arteriole. The pressure of the blood in the afferent arteriole is 70 mm Hg. Inside the glomerulus, this pressure balances at 50 mm Hg. This glomerular pressure encourages the passage of ultrafiltrate. Ultrafiltrate is the fluid that travels from the glomerular space to Bowman's capsule and into the tubules. Two forces oppose the formation of filtrate: colloid osmotic pressure (a pressure of 25 mm Hg exerted by the plasma proteins located in the glomerular blood supply) and Bowman's capsule pressure (a pressure of 10 mm Hg produced by the tissue encompassing the glomerulus). Subtracting these opposing factors from the capillary pressure results in a net filtration pressure of 15 mm Hg.

The positive force of the net pressure promotes the movement of fluid and solute across the glomerular membrane. The glomerular membrane is semipermeable to allow the passage of water and most solutes in the blood, such as glucose, sodium, and metabolic wastes. Larger molecules, such as plasma proteins, erythrocytes, leukocytes, and platelets, are effectively restricted by the glomerular membrane.

Tubular Reabsorption

Urine formation in the tubules begins as the filtrate enters the proximal tubule. The primary function of the proximal tubule is reabsorption. Reabsorption of 60% to 80% of essential water and proteins occurs at this point (Figure 2-3).

Tubular reabsorption involves active and passive transport mechanisms. Substances that require energy to move against a concentration gradient are actively transported, for example, glucose, phosphate, amino acids, sodium, and potassium. Other substances such as water, urea, and chloride are passively reabsorbed (require no energy).

Tubular Secretion

The process of tubular secretion involves both active and passive mechanisms. The two most common electrolytes secreted are hydrogen and potassium. Other substances secreted by the tubules include ammonia, uric acid, and exogenous substances (e.g., drugs).

ACID-BASE BALANCE

Acid-base balance is regulated by the chemical buffer system, the respiratory system, and the kidney.

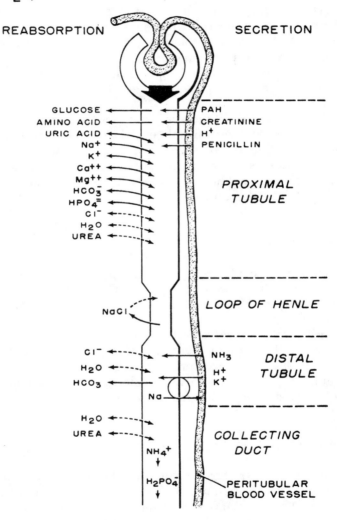

Figure 2-3 Tubular reabsorption and secretion. *Source:* Reproduced by permission from S.A. Price and L.M. Wilson, *Pathophysiology*, 3rd ed., 1986, New York: McGraw-Hill. Copyright 1986 by The C.V. Mosby Company, St. Louis.

Chemical Buffer System

Chemical buffers are present in all body fluids. Acid-base buffers combine with any acid or alkali to prevent excessive changes in hydrogen ion concentration.

The pH of the plasma is determined by the ratio of sodium bicarbonate to carbonic acid, the principal buffer pair. Because the body has a stronger tendency toward acidity, it requires a more basic than acidic buffering system. The end product of cellular metabolism is carbon dioxide (acid). When combined with water, carbonic acid is formed: $CO_2 + H_2O \rightarrow H_2CO_3$. The ratio of bicarbonate (base) to carbonic acid is normally 20:1.

The sodium bicarbonate–carbonic acid buffer system is responsible for approximately 45% of all hydrogen ion buffering. Hydrochloric acid (HCl), a strong acid, reacts with sodium bicarbonate ($NaHCO_3$) to convert the strong acid to a weak one—carbonic acid (H_2CO_3). Carbonic acid then dissociates into carbon dioxide (CO_2) and water (H_2O).

Respiratory Regulation

The CO_2 formed by the dissociation of H_2CO_3 is transferred to the lungs, where it diffuses into the alveoli and is eliminated by exhalation. The rate of alveolar ventilation affects hydrogen ion concentration in body fluids. As alveolar ventilation increases, CO_2 is blown off and the pH increases; as alveolar ventilation decreases, the pH decreases. Hydrogen ion concentration also affects the rate of ventilation. Circulating hydrogen ions in the plasma stimulate the respiratory center of the medulla oblongata, which increases ventilation.

Renal Regulation

The kidney regulates acid-base balance by the secretion of hydrogen ions, the reabsorption and generation of bicarbonate, and the production of ammonia.

The kidney regulates hydrogen ion concentration by increasing or decreasing the bicarbonate concentration in body fluids by a series of complex chemical reactions that occur in the renal tubules. The hydrogen ions secreted into the tubular fluid are eliminated in the urine as water in combination with ammonia. Sodium ions are reabsorbed from the tubular fluid into the extracellular fluid in exchange for hydrogen ions, and combine with bicarbonate to form the buffer sodium bicarbonate.

Secretion of hydrogen ions into the glomerular filtrate actually begins in the tubular cells of the proximal and distal tubules as well as in the collecting duct and thick portion of the loop of Henle. $CO_2 + H_2O$, facilitated by carbonic anhydrase, yields H_2CO_3. The carbonic acid dissociates into H^+ and HCO_3^-. The hydrogen ion is secreted via active transport from the cell into the tubule. There it combines with HCO_3^- and forms H_2CO_3, which dissociates into H_2O and CO_2. Hydrogen in the form of H_2O is eliminated from the body as urine.

Sodium ions found within the tubular fluid are actively reabsorbed into the peritubular capillaries surrounding the nephron. Generally, one sodium ion is reabsorbed for every hydrogen ion secreted. Bicarbonate ions form within the cells as a result of the breakdown of carbonic acid diffusion into the blood and combine with sodium ions, forming the buffer sodium bicarbonate.

When excess hydrogen ions are secreted into the tubules, only a small amount can be excreted in the urine. The excess hydrogen ions must combine with buffer compounds found in the tubular fluid. Two important buffer systems responsible for eliminating excess hydrogen ions in the urine are phosphate buffers and ammonia buffers. Excess hydrogen ions enter the tubules and combine with phosphate, which is then eliminated in the urine. When glutamine (an amino acid found within the cells) is metabolized, ammonia is formed, which diffuses into the tubular fluid. There it combines with excess hydrogen ions to form ammonium ions (NH_4), which are then excreted in the urine.

EXCRETION OF METABOLIC WASTE PRODUCTS

The excretion of metabolic waste products is a primary renal function. Among the substances excreted daily are metabolic end products, excess levels of hormones, environmental wastes, and pharmacologic agents. Blood urea nitrogen (BUN) and serum creatinine are the two waste products measured for interpretation of renal function. Urea is a nitrogenous waste product of protein metabolism that is filtered and reabsorbed along the nephron (Stark, 1980). BUN is influenced by extrarenal factors such as dehydration, drug metabolism, catabolic rate, and hypoperfusion states. An increase in BUN without a corresponding increase in creatinine or an increase in the BUN-to-creatinine ratio of 20:1 is indicative of hypovolemia, renal hypoperfusion, and increased catabolic rate. An elevation of both BUN and creatinine in a 10:1 ratio is indicative of renal disease.

Serum creatinine measurement can be used as a true assessment of renal function. Creatinine is a waste product of muscle metabolism and is continuously produced and continuously excreted by the kidneys. The normal kidney can rid the body of daily creatinine loads. Elevations in creatinine above the normal 0.6 to 1.2 mg/dL are associated with renal disease.

REGULATION OF BLOOD PRESSURE

The kidney regulates blood pressure via three mechanisms: (1) sodium and water regulation, (2) angiotensin action, and (3) prostaglandin secretion.

Sodium and Water Regulation

The kidney maintains the volume and composition of the extracellular fluid. Any change in plasma volume affects cardiac output and blood pressure.

Angiotensin Action

The renin-angiotensin-aldosterone system is a governing mechanism that maintains systemic blood pressure and protects against important volume losses. Renin is stored in and released from the juxtaglomerular apparatus (Figure 2-4). This apparatus is composed of juxtaglomerular cells and the macula densa. The juxtaglomerular cells are located within the afferent arteriole and are positioned adjacent to the glomerulus. Hypotension, hypovolemia, and hyponatremia are the three primary stimulants of renin release. Position changes (e.g., moving from a lying to a sitting position) and life stressors also stimulate renin release.

After being stimulated, the juxtaglomerular cells release renin into the circulation. Renin acts on angiotensinogen, a plasma-borne substrate synthesized by the liver, to form angiotensin I. Angiotensin I is converted to angiotensin II by a converting enzyme. Most of the conversion occurs in the lung tissue. Some conversion also takes place in renal and liver tissue as well as in vessel walls.

Angiotensin II is the active element of the catalytic action of renin. It is a potent peripheral vasoconstrictor and stimulator of aldosterone secretion. Angiotensin II has a direct vasoconstrictive effect on vascular smooth muscle. Systemic vasoconstriction maintains blood pressure in states of severe sodium depletion of extracellular fluid loss. Renal arteriolar constriction results in retention of sodium and water by the kidney. This volume expansion causes the blood pressure to increase.

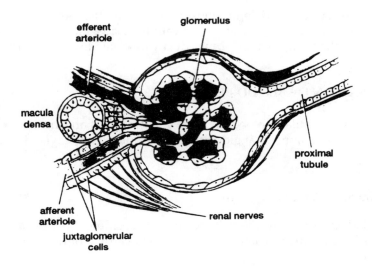

Figure 2-4 Juxtaglomerular apparatus. *Source:* From *Human Physiology*, 2nd ed. (p. 519), by A.J. Vander, J.H. Sherman, and D. Luciano, 1975, New York: McGraw-Hill. Copyright 1975 by McGraw-Hill. Reprinted by permission.

Circulating blood volume is effectively restored by angiotensin II stimulation of the zona glomerulosa cells to release aldosterone. Aldosterone increases renal tubular reabsorption of hydrogen at the distal tubule and collecting ducts. Potassium and hydrogen ions are selectively secreted into the tubular fluid in exchange for the reabsorbed sodium ions. The release of aldosterone results in a significant expansion of plasma volume by sodium and water retention, thus elevating systemic blood pressure (Figure 2-5).

Prostaglandin Secretion

Prostaglandins are unsaturated fatty acids made by most tissues in the body. Five prostaglandins are known to be produced by the kidney, three that are vasodilative and two that are vasoconstrictive.

The secretion of vasodilative prostaglandins is triggered by the release of any vasoactive substance, such as angiotensin II. Prostaglandins regulate the effects of all of the vasoactive substances. For example, the degree of vasoconstriction caused by angiotensin II can be controlled by the

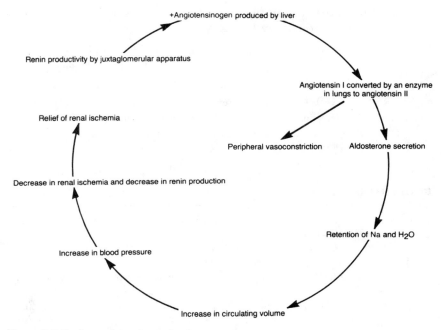

Figure 2-5 Renin-angiotensin mechanism.

vasodilative prostaglandins. The vasodilative actions of substances such as bradykinin are enhanced by the vasodilative prostaglandins.

CONVERSION OF VITAMIN D$_3$

The kidney extracts 25-dihydroxyvitamin D$_3$ (inactive form) and converts it to 1,25-dihydroxyvitamin D$_3$ (active form), then releases the product into the blood stream. On entering the blood stream, 1,25-dihydroxyvitamin D$_3$ is carried to the intestine, where it stimulates calcium absorption, and to bones, where it promotes calcium mobilization.

ERYTHROPOIETIN SECRETION

Erythropoietin is a hormone necessary for the production and maintenance of new erythrocytes. It is secreted by renal tissues in response to a decrease in renal oxygen supply. Erythropoietin acts on bone marrow to enhance the production of erythrocytes.

REFERENCES

Fairchild, R.S. (1980). Diabetes insipidus: A review. *Critical Care Quarterly, 2*(3), 111–118.

Stark, J. (1980). BUN/creatinine: Your keys to kidney function. *Nursing '80, 10*(5), 30–38.

Stark, J. (1985). The renal system. In J. Alspach & S. Williams, Eds., *Core curriculum for critical care nursing*. Philadelphia: Saunders.

SUGGESTED READINGS

Chambers, J.E. (1987). Fluid and electrolyte problems in renal and urologic disorders. *Nursing Clinics of North America, 22*, 815–826.

Chevney, B. (1987). Overview of fluids and electrolytes. *Nursing Clinics of North America, 22*, 749–759.

Hekelman, F.P., & Ostendarp, C.A. (1979). *Nephrology nursing perspectives of care*. New York: McGraw-Hill.

Lancaster, L.E. (1987). Anatomy and physiology of the renal system. In L.E. Lancaster (Ed.), *Core curriculum for nephrology nursing*. Pitman, NJ: American Nephrology Nurses' Association.

Lancaster, L.E. (1987). Renal and endocrine regulation of water and electrolyte balance. *Nursing Clinics of North America, 22*, 761–772.

Lindbloom, L. (1982). Fluid and electrolyte balance. In E. Larson, L. Lindbloom, & K.B. Davis (Eds.), *Development of the clinical nephrology practitioner: A focus on independent learning*. St. Louis: Mosby.

Schoengrund, L., & Balzer, P. (Eds.). (1985). *Renal problems in critical care*. New York: Wiley.

Stark, J.L. (1988). Renal anatomy and physiology. In M.R. Kinney, D.R. Packa, & S.B. Dunbar (Eds.), *AACN's clinical reference for critical care nursing* (2nd ed.). New York: McGraw-Hill.

3

Renal Assessment

Renal assessment should include a history, a physical examination, analysis of laboratory data, a radiologic examination, and (if indicated) renal biopsy.

HISTORY

A complete history should be taken and should elicit information about the following:

- family history of renal disease (polycystic kidney disease, renal calculi, diabetes mellitus, gout, malignant disease, hereditary nephritis, hypertension, and cardiovascular disease)
- history of acute or chronic renal failure or urinary tract disease
- history of cardiovascular disease (e.g., congestive heart failure)
- history of hypertensive disease or atherosclerosis
- history of diabetes mellitus (Diabetes mellitus can contribute to different forms of glomerular disease, pyelonephritis, papillary necrosis, and accelerated arteriolar sclerosis.)
- history of streptococcal infections (Streptococcal infections can cause glomerular disease.)
- history of recurrent urinary tract infection (UTI) (Particular attention should be given to the causative organism and a history of recurrence; the same organism may suggest infection of the kidney or prostate; variation in the organism may reflect a bladder infection [Ronald, 1983].)
- history of renal calculi

- concurrent or recent pulmonary disease and renal related disease (Such patients should be evaluated for Goodpasture syndrome, an autoimmune disorder in which antibodies attack both the lung and the kidney.)
- pregnancy in the presence of diabetes mellitus or hypertension
- history of renal transplant complications associated with acute or chronic rejection, and immunosuppressive side effects
- history of exposure to nephrotoxic agents

PHYSICAL EXAMINATION

The objective of the physical examination is to review the body systems for data that may contribute to a diagnosis of renal disease.

General Appearance

The patient's general appearance should be assessed for signs of malaise, fatigue, or weight loss or gain.

Integument

Skin color is abnormal in both acute and chronic renal failure. The skin may be grayish and pale (related to anemia) or have a yellowish tinge caused by the retention of carotenoids (related to uremia).

Bruising, petechiae, and ecchymoses due to increased capillary fragility; purpuric lesions; and abnormal clotting caused by uremia may be noted. The patient may exhibit scratch marks resulting from the chronic pruritus related to uremia.

The skin texture may be rough or scaly; uremia is thought to atrophy the skin's oil and sweat glands. The patient may have uremic frost, a film that coats the skin's surface; it is caused by the passage of urate crystals through the pores.

Edema in the extremities, lungs, and periorbital area suggests retention of sodium and water.

Nails may be brittle and thin and crack easily (associated with malnutrition in renal disease).

Hair texture may be altered as a result of malnutrition in renal disease. The hair may be dry, and the patient may have some hair loss.

Head, Ears, Eyes, Nose, Throat

The eyes may have band keratopathy—white bands seen across the cornea, caused by chronic hypercalcemia associated with renal disease.

The mucous membranes of the nose and mouth may exhibit swelling, redness, and ulcerations with toxic anemia; pallor may indicate anemia; uremic fetor or odor to the breath is associated with uremia.

Nerve deafness caused by antibiotic toxicity or hereditary nephropathy may be present.

Lungs

Infection is a primary concern with uremia. Uremia impairs the immune response of the lungs and suppresses the cough reflex. Patients with these deficits may exhibit thick, tenacious sputum; fever; and an irregular respiratory rate. The lungs may have abnormal auscultatory sounds of crackles or wheezes. Two specific conditions seen are Goodpasture syndrome and uremic lung.

Goodpasture Syndrome

Goodpasture syndrome is an autoimmune disorder in which antibodies attack both the lung and the kidney. The patient with Goodpasture syndrome will have a history of a recent respiratory infection. Assessment will reveal hemoptysis, orthopnea, dyspnea, or crackles. Jugular vein distention (JVD) may accompany congestive heart failure. Pulmonary hemorrhage may cause crackles.

Uremic Lung

Uremic lung is manifested by interstitial edema and respiratory failure. The patient exhibits dyspnea, labored respirations, and crackles. A chest x-ray will demonstrate a butterfly configuration, indicating respiratory failure.

Cardiovascular System

Renal disease causes a variety of problems in the cardiovascular system. Hypertension, pericarditis, and atherosclerosis are some of the most common problems.

Hypertension

Hypertension may be present as a result of volume expansion.

Pericarditis

Pericarditis may have an onset that coincides with a uremic exacerbation. The patient will present with pain, shortness of breath, and fever. Other symptoms include a pericardial friction rub and ST elevation on the electrocardiogram (Rose, 1981). Cardiac tamponade is a complication. The nurse should observe for pulsus paradoxus, hypotension, and JVD.

Atherosclerosis

Atherosclerosis may be present and cause a variety of symptoms. The uremic patient is in a hyperlipidemic state, which contributes to atherosclerosis. Uremia may accelerate the atherosclerotic process.

Congestive Heart Failure

Congestive heart failure results from fluid overload. The patient may have an S_3 heart sound, shortness of breath, JVD, pitting edema in the lower extremities, cold/clammy skin, decreased urine output, and altered mental status.

Neuromuscular System

Usually problems in the neuromuscular system are caused by acid-base or electrolyte imbalances. Uremia causes uremic encephalopathy and peripheral neuropathy. The patient with uremic encephalopathy may exhibit changes in mental status that range from lethargy to coma. Other neurologic manifestations associated with uremia include seizures, diminished coordination, tremors, and asterixis.

Peripheral neuropathy progresses from the lower extremities to the upper extremities. The nerves undergo segmental demyelination. Results of the physical examination will vary depending on the stage of peripheral neuropathy. Initially, the patient may experience "restless leg syndrome," usually when he or she is at rest. The patient relieves pain by moving the legs in a restless pattern. Burning pain with varying intensity may be felt on the dorsal and ventral surfaces of the feet. This syndrome may progress to foot drop and paralysis. Electrolyte imbalances may cause some neurologic symptoms (e.g., hypocalcemia may cause muscle twitching).

Skeletal System

Bone disease may include osteomalacia and osteitis fibrosa. The patient may have bone pain and activity intolerance. He or she may be susceptible to spontaneous fractures. Bone demineralization may also occur.

Gastrointestinal System

A variety of problems may be manifested, including anorexia, nausea/vomiting, abdominal distention, stomatitis, and uremic fetor.

Renal disease may also precipitate peptic and stress ulcers. Stools and emesis should be assessed for the presence of occult blood.

Patients with chronic renal failure have a condition known as "uremic bowel." It is manifested by alternating periods of diarrhea and constipation.

Amyloidosis may be manifested by an enlarged liver or spleen.

Genitourinary System

Kidney Size

The right kidney should be palpated to assess shape and size and to detect tenderness or masses. The patient should be instructed to take a deep breath while the examiner reaches under the rib cage and attempts to palpate the lower pole of the right kidney. Inability to palpate may indicate small or atrophied kidneys. Palpation of a large kidney suggests diseases such as polycystic kidney disease.

Kidney Pain

Pain that originates in the anterior or posterior portion of the kidney and radiates toward the groin is characteristic of ureter involvement. Ureteric colic may be caused by renal calculi or thrombi.

Urinary Symptoms

Pain anywhere in the urinary tract is usually accompanied by complaints of urgency, frequency, and hesitancy. Urine color may be reported as grossly bloody, cloudy, or orange (associated with bilirubinuria). The patient may also report nocturia, polyuria, incontinence, oliguria, or anuria.

Fever

Fever accompanied by pain usually indicates pyelonephritis (acute episode) or cystitis. Renal calculi are manifested by pain accompanied by an enlarged renal pelvis.

Blood and Blood-Forming Tissues

Anemia secondary to decreased erythropoietin secretion is common. The hematocrit typically is around 20%. Indications for transfusion are pallor, fatigue, activity intolerance, shortness of breath, and chest pain.

Endocrine System

Several hormones are thought to contribute to the development of uremic symptoms. Parathyroid hormone is probably a primary factor in the skeletal and sexual dysfunction associated with uremia.

ANALYSIS OF LABORATORY DATA

Creatinine

Creatinine reflects glomerular filtration rate (GFR). Creatinine is a product of muscle metabolism. It is produced daily in proportion to muscle mass (which is relatively stable from day to day). A normal value is 0.5 to 1.5 mg/dL. Renal failure reflects the kidney's inability to excrete creatinine, with a consequent elevation of serum levels.

Blood Urea Nitrogen

Blood urea nitrogen (BUN) is an end product of protein breakdown. The rate of protein metabolism varies according to protein intake and the degree of catabolism caused by undernutrition, reabsorption of a hematoma, infection, steroids, surgery, and use of medications (Stark, 1980). Excessive protein metabolism may increase BUN levels despite a normal GFR. For example, a burn victim may be catabolic and exhibit an increased BUN level with normal renal function. A decrease in GFR leads to an increase in BUN concentration without a change in the serum creatinine level. An extrarenal problem, excessive protein metabolism, dehydration, or a decrease in renal perfusion state increases the BUN-to-serum creatinine ratio to greater than 20:1. Renal failure (acute and chronic) increases the ratio of BUN to creatinine to 10:1 (e.g., BUN = 100 mg/dL; creatinine = 10 mg/dL).

Creatinine Clearance

Creatinine clearance reflects the percentage of functioning nephrons. It is measured by a 24-hour urine collection. The formula for calculating creatinine clearance is as follows:

$$UCR \times V/PCR$$
where UCR = urine creatinine, V = volume of urine, and PCR = plasma creatinine

The normal value for creatinine clearance is 110 to 120 mL/min.

Urinalysis

Urinalysis can be helpful in establishing a diagnosis. Examination of urine should be done on a freshly voided specimen.

Physical Analysis

Color. Urine is normally pale yellow to amber. Color changes usually occur as a result of three factors: (a) an increase in metabolites excreted in the urine, (b) substances in the urine that reflect renal or urinary tract disorders, and (c) dietary/medication substances. Gross hematuria is shown by urine that is red-colored. Myoglobin and free hemoglobin may cause the red color. Phenolsulfonphthalein, a diagnostic dye, will cause alkaline urine to turn red. Red blood cells and heme pigments may cause urine color to range from pink to black. Malignant melanoma may cause the pigment melanogen to be deposited, causing the urine to turn black. Patients with obstructive jaundice will have a variation in urine color ranging from yellow to brown or green, caused by the presence of bile salts. Methylene blue and azure A dyes cause urine to turn blue. Phenazopyridine hydrochloride (Pyridium) causes urine to turn orange. Food dyes, riboflavin, and multivitamins may cause the urine to have a bright yellow color.

Clarity. Urine should be clear. Cloudiness in a freshly voided urine specimen may indicate the presence of epithelial cells or leukocytes. Cloudy urine is usually associated with UTI, since bacteria can cause cloudiness. Amorphous phosphate particles precipitate in acid or alkaline urine, causing cloudiness. Mucus causes a hazy appearance; fat causes a murky appearance; and red blood cells that collect in urine cause a turbid appearance.

Odor

Odor may provide a clue about urine content. Ketones in the urine produce a sweet, fruity odor. Excess methionine in the urine causes a fishy odor. Butyric or hexanoic acid causes a foul odor to the urine.

Specific Gravity

Specific gravity indicates the density of dissolved substances in the urine. Serial specific gravity values demonstrate the kidney's ability to concentrate or dilute the urine. Normal urine specific gravity is 1.003 to 1.030. The kidney adjusts specific gravity throughout the day as it responds to the body's water balance. Values that are falsely high may be caused by the presence of radiopaque dye. Glucose or protein in large amounts may lead to a high specific gravity (greater than 1.030). Dehydration, eclampsia, and lipid nephrosis may also cause a high specific gravity.

A low specific gravity may be caused by overhydration, diuretic therapy, and coffee or alcohol consumption. Certain diseases may be associated with low specific gravity, such as hypertension, pyelonephritis, diabetes insipidus, or hypoproteinemic conditions.

Osmolality is a more accurate indicator of the kidney's ability to concentrate or dilute urine. Specific gravity is changed by the presence of proteins, cell casts, and other substances; osmolality is not affected by these substances.

pH. Normal pH values range from 4.5 to 8.0 in response to the kidney's changes in acid-base balance and the urinary excretion of alkalies or acids. Normal urine is usually acid since daily dietary consumptions create metabolites that are acid. Ingestion of fruits and proteins results in an acid urine. Undernutrition, diabetic ketosis, severe diarrhea, hyperkalemia, and respiratory alkalosis also produce an acid urine. UTI caused by *Escherichia coli* results in an acid urine.

Regulation of urine pH is beneficial in preventing renal calculus formation and in suppressing chronic urinary tract infections. The administration of ammonium chloride, mandelic acid, or ascorbic acid maintains an acid urine, thus decreasing the chances that alkaline renal stones will form.

The administration of sodium bicarbonate, acetazolamide, or potassium citrate maintains an alkaline urine, which may reduce the incidence of some UTIs, and may prevent the development of renal stones formed from uric acid, calcium oxalate, or cystine.

Proteinuria. Normal urine should not contain protein. However, the urine of some patients may have a trace of protein. High levels of protein and albumin in the urine suggest some type of renal or urinary tract disease.

Functional proteinuria is defined as a total protein content of 150 mg to 1 g/24 hours and is associated with nonrenal causes, including stress, aggressive exercise, febrile states, and exposure to extreme temperature changes. This type of proteinuria is reversible.

A consistently elevated urinary protein level is associated with nephrotic syndrome, glomerulonephritis, lupus nephritis, and amyloidosis. Lower levels of proteinuria ranging from 1 to 3.5 g/24 hours are associated with diabetic nephropathy, hypertension, polycystic kidney disease, and chronic pyelonephritis.

Proteinuria associated with UTI usually indicates an infection in the upper urinary tract because infections in this area affect glomerular function, resulting in protein excretion.

Microscopic Analysis of Urinary Sediment

Particles composed of casts, cells, crystals, and some miscellaneous materials make up urinary sediment. Urinary casts are molded in the lumina of the tubules. They begin as cells or other substances. Proteinuria, acidosis, and a high concentration of urine cause an increase in cast formation. Cast types include hyaline, red blood cell, white blood cell, epithelial cell, granular, waxy, fatty, and renal tubular. Alterations in renal function reflect the amount and type of cast formed.

Hyaline Casts. Hyaline casts are composed of protein and appear more often in the urine than do other casts. Normal urine may contain small amounts of hyaline casts. Extremely vigorous exercise and hypovolemic states may cause hyaline casts to appear in the urine.

Red Blood Cell Casts. Red blood cell casts are abnormal. The urine will appear brown or red-tinged. Disease states associated with the presence of red blood cell casts include glomerulonephritis, renal trauma, pyelonephritis, bacterial endocarditis, renal infarction, and renal vein thrombosis.

White Blood Cell Casts. White blood cell casts are associated with renal infection or inflammation, or both. Renal diseases associated with white blood cell casts are pyelonephritis, lupus nephritis, and interstitial nephritis.

Epithelial Cell Casts. Epithelial cell casts are caused by damage to the renal tubules resulting from a nephrotoxic injury, allergic reaction, viral insult, ischemia, or transplant rejection. Epithelial cell casts are also seen in some forms of chronic renal failure.

Granular Casts. Granular casts are normally present in small amounts in urine. They are caused by the breakdown of other cellular casts (white or red blood cell casts) or the clumping of serum proteins. Large numbers of granular casts indicate renal disease.

Waxy Casts. Waxy casts are thought to result from degraded cellular casts. Chronic and acute renal failure, malignant hypertension, and renal transplant rejection are conditions associated with waxy casts.

Fatty Casts. Fatty casts contain lipid material. The degradation of fatty substances in the tubular wall causes fatty cast formation. Tubular dysfunction such as occurs in lipoid nephrosis, nephrotic syndrome, glomerulonephropathies, and nephrotoxic episodes is associated with the presence of fatty casts.

Renal Tubular Casts. Renal tubular casts result from tubular injury. Ischemia or nephrotoxicity causes tubular cells to be degraded. The cells fall into the tubular space and assume the shape of the space in which they aggregate.

RADIOLOGIC EXAMINATION

A radiologic examination assists in determining the existence and extent of renal and urinary tract disease. Various tests reveal the renal system's structure, function, and blood supply. Tests are selected based on the type of information needed to make a diagnosis, risks of the examination, and dependability of the test results.

Intravenous Pyelogram

The intravenous pyelogram (IVP) enables visualization of the kidney and urinary tract via injection of radiocontrast dye. The calices, renal pelvis, ureters, and bladder are visible with this test. Adequate visibility of the urinary tract allows the diagnosis of partial obstruction, renovascular hypertension, tumors, cysts, and congenital abnormalities (Stark, 1985). Hydronephrosis may also be detected with the IVP.

The IVP contrast dye may cause nephrotoxicity. In some patients, it may cause renal failure. The IVP dye causes a hyperosmotic state in the plasma, which results in diuresis and precipitates a state of dehydration. Dehydration in combination with the nephrotoxic effects of the dye in a patient with renal failure may exacerbate the severity of the renal disease. Administration of several liters of fluid prior to, during, and after the procedure may help prevent dehydration and decrease the toxicity of the dye by dilution and enhanced excretion.

The IVP is contraindicated in patients with multiple myeloma, diabetes mellitus, or congestive heart failure and in pregnant patients. The IVP dye promotes sickling and renal infarction in patients with sickle cell disease.

Radiography of Kidneys, Ureter, and Bladder

Radiography of kidneys, ureter, and bladder has a low risk to a patient. It may be the first test used to study the renal system. A radiograph of the kidneys, ureter, and bladder reveals the position, size, and shape of the kidneys. Sometimes renal calculi and masses are visible.

The size of the kidneys is important diagnostically. An acute process may be indicated by bilateral kidney enlargement. Polycystic kidney disease and amyloidosis are chronic conditions that also cause kidney enlargement. Small kidneys usually indicate chronic disease.

A small kidney unilaterally may result from pyelonephritis and renal artery stenosis. A large kidney unilaterally may occur secondary to obstruction, acute renal vein thrombosis, or a renal mass.

Renal Scan

A renal scan is a radionuclide study that measures renal perfusion and function. It also reveals the presence of obstruction and renal masses. It assists in determining the degree of renal ischemia caused by acute tubular necrosis or renal transplantation. Kidney function is assessed through the rate of uptake and excretion of radioisotopes. The radionuclide material is excreted in the urine.

Retrograde Pyelogram

A retrograde pyelogram allows visualization of the ureters and the upper area of the urinary tract. Catheters are passed into the ureters and radiopaque dye is injected. A retrograde pyelogram allows the diagnosis of partial and complete obstruction.

Arteriography

Arteriography allows visualization of renal vasculature to assess for renal artery stenosis, or to differentiate a benign cyst from a carcinoma. Radiocontrast dye is injected directly into the aorta near the bifurcation of the renal arteries, or into the renal arteries.

Risks with this test are similar to those associated with IVP with respect to reactions to dye. Other possible complications include laceration of the renal artery, hematoma formation, embolism, or thrombosis.

Ultrasonography

Ultrasonography allows visualization of the renal system through an imaging technique. Ultrasonography has a very low risk and therefore is excellent for patients with contrast media allergies and for those who are critically ill and unable to tolerate a more invasive procedure.

Ultrasonography provides reliable data about the size and shape of the kidneys, which assist in assessment for renal cysts, abscesses, tumors, and polycystic kidney disease. It is also beneficial in diagnosing lymphoceles and intrarenal or extrarenal hemorrhage in renal transplant recipients (Holmes, 1983).

This test is valuable in assessing urinary tract obstruction in an anuric patient. Hydronephrosis can also be diagnosed since calices are easily visualized.

Computed Tomography

Computed tomography provides an exact anatomic view of the kidney's retroperitoneal space, the urinary bladder, and the prostate gland. Other anomalies of size and shape, including horseshoe and polycystic kidneys, can also be identified.

Magnetic Resonance Imaging

Magnetic resonance imaging provides data without x-radiation similar to those provided by computed tomography. Magnetic resonance imaging studies the chemical structure of intact tissues by detecting frequency peaks representative of the chemical composition of each nucleus (Weiner & Adam, 1985). These peaks represent normal or abnormal cell function. Metabolic disturbances caused by ischemic or acid-base imbalances or tumor growth may be detected by magnetic resonance imaging.

RENAL BIOPSY

Renal biopsy is the most invasive test that may be performed as an open or closed procedure. The open technique is used when gross anatomic deformities exist or when a deep specimen is needed, as for determining the presence of polyarteritis nodosa or dense deposit disease.

For the closed technique, the kidney's position is established by fluoroscopy or ultrasonography. A posterior approach is used for insertion of the biopsy needle.

The primary complication of both biopsy approaches is localized bleeding. It is very important that the biopsy site be examined immediately after the procedure for swelling and localized bleeding manifested by changes in skin color. Frequent blood pressure monitoring is necessary for 2 to 4 hours after the biopsy, as well as hematocrit assessment. Wound infection may be a complication with an open biopsy.

REFERENCES

Holmes, J.H. (1983). Diagnostic use of ultrasound for kidney and bladder. In S.G. Massey & R.J. Glasscock (Eds.), *Textbook of nephrology* (Vol. 2, pp. 1211–1219). Baltimore: Williams & Wilkins.

Ronald, A.R. (1983). The management of urethrocystitis in women. *Seminars in Urology, 1*(2), 114–120.

Rose, D.B. (1981). *Pathophysiology of renal disease* (pp. 448–449). New York: McGraw-Hill.

Stark, J. (1980). BUN/creatinine: Your keys to kidney function. *Nursing '80, 10*(5), 30–38.

Stark, J. (1985). The renal system. In J. Alspach & S. Williams (Eds.), *Core curriculum for critical care nursing* (pp. 347–448). Philadelphia: Saunders.

Weiner, M.W., & Adam, W.R. (1985). Magnetic resonance spectroscopy for evaluation of renal function. *Seminars in Urology, 3*(1), 34–42.

SUGGESTED READINGS

Richard, C.J. (1987). Assessment of renal structure and function. In L.E. Lancaster (Ed.), *Core curriculum for nephrology nursing*. Pitman, NJ: American Nephrology Nurses' Association.

Schoengrund, L., & Balzer, P. (Eds.). (1985). *Renal problems in critical care.* New York: Wiley.

Stark, J.L. (1988). Renal anatomy and physiology. In M.R. Kinney, D.R. Packa, & S.B. Dunbar (Eds.), *AACN's clinical reference for critical care nursing* (2nd ed.). New York: McGraw-Hill.

4

Renal Failure

ACUTE RENAL FAILURE

Acute renal failure (ARF) is defined as the sudden cessation of renal function, which may have many causes. ARF results from prerenal, intrarenal, and postrenal conditions.

Prerenal ARF

Prerenal ARF results from a decreased perfusion of the kidney without renal tubular damage. The glomerular filtration rate decreases and is reflected by a decrease in urine output; the nephrons remain intact.

Several conditions cause prerenal ARF, ranging from hypovolemia to impaired cardiac function to vascular dynamic changes. Most forms of prerenal ARF are easily reversed. The goal is to improve renal perfusion through volume replacement, enhanced cardiac output, or reversal of vasoconstriction or vasodilatation.

Prerenal conditions may be divided into two categories in terms of risk to the patient for development of intrarenal kidney damage. Conditions that respond quickly to treatment and are easily reversed can be considered mild forms of prerenal failure. Stark (1988) described mild prerenal failure as follows:

> An example of mild prerenal failure is uncomplicated dehydration. The nurse would notice during this condition a decrease in urine output over several hours or the eventual absence of output. This change in renal function should be correlated with recent negative intake/output balance, weight loss, hypotension, decreased neck veins, low central venous pressure, decreased

wedge pressure, dry mucous membranes, and alteration in mental status, usually lethargy. An examination of recent lab studies would reveal an elevated serum BUN [blood urea nitrogen] and normal or slightly elevated creatinine in a greater than 20:1 ratio. A spot urine sodium would reveal a value of 10 mEq or less. All of these findings would support the presence of dehydration. A fluid challenge and then the initiation of volume replacement therapy with a solution comparable to the type lost restores urine output. Conditions such as this would respond to immediate treatment of the primary cause by restoration of the renal function. (p. 874)

High-risk conditions are those in which the kidneys are in a hypoperfused state for an extended period (e.g., as in cardiogenic shock). The patient who has experienced multiple trauma, cardiogenic shock, or hemodynamic instability often has a slow response to treatment, and acute tubular necrosis (ATN) develops. A nonoliguric type of ATN has a better chance of being reversed. Treatment goals are to increase renal perfusion and reverse altered renal hemodynamics. Altered renal hemodynamics may be reversed by expanding volume with a colloidal solution (e.g., plasma) (Burke & Schrier, 1983; Hsu & Kurtz, 1981; Maher, 1981). If the use of colloidal solutions is inappropriate, saline or Ringer's lactate may be used. These methods improve cardiac output, which will directly improve renal perfusion (Stark, 1985).

If volume expansion is not achievable or is inadequate, medications may be used to improve renal blood flow, including vasodilators (e.g., dopamine), to improve renal blood flow and to improve glomerular filtration rate, and diuretics (e.g., furosemide), to prevent possible tubular obstruction and to increase urine flow. Other blood flow augmentors include mannitol, prostaglandins, bradykinins, and ethacrynic acid.

Intrarenal ARF

Intrarenal ARF is caused by damage to the glomeruli, vessels, or tubules. Tubular damage is slow and may require a year for healing. ATN is the most common cause of intrarenal ARF.

Acute Tubular Necrosis

ATN results from either nephrotoxic or ischemic injury. Antibiotics, specifically the aminoglycosides, are the most common cause of nephrotoxic injury (Goldstein, 1983). The epithelial layer of the tubule has the ability to regenerate. Healing occurs quickly with this type of injury (10 days to 2 weeks without complications). ATN resulting from hypotensive occurrences, infection, and dehydration may increase the nephrotoxic damage (Kon & Ichikawa, 1984; Mars & Treloar, 1984).

Patients who are at high risk for developing ATN are those with hemodynamic instability, severe multiple trauma, prolonged surgery, or burns. Contrast dye is the second most common cause of ATN. Other causes of nephrotoxic injury are heavy metals and endogenous toxins such as myoglobin secondary to rhabdomyolysis, septic endotoxins, and hemoglobin post-transfusion reaction. Administering large volumes of intravenous fluids before, during, or after a test procedure may prevent or minimize the nephrotoxic injury.

ATN resulting in ischemic injury suggests a prerenal state that is unresolved. The implementation of therapeutic modalities to augment blood flow determines whether the patient will begin ARF in oliguria or nonoliguria (Conger, 1983; Wilson & Brackett, 1983). ATN is often manifested by oliguria resulting from one of two physiologic events, intratubular obstruction or back leak phenomenon.

Intratubular Obstruction. In intratubular obstruction, tubular cells slough off in response to the ischemic incident and collect in the tubular space. In order to remove the intratubular obstruction and restore tubular patency, large boluses of diuretics may be given at the onset of ATN.

Back Leak Phenomenon. In back leak phenomenon, the tubular wall develops "cracks" as a result of the ischemic event. The filtrate leaks into the body, resulting in a decreased urine output and oliguria.

The patient with an oliguric ATN will have increased biochemical values secondary to a decreased creatinine clearance. Hyperkalemia is the most serious condition to observe. Hyperkalemia results from catabolism, hemolysis, tissue breakdown, and endogenous causes. A potassium level greater than 6.0 mEq/L may involve the cardiac system. Acidemia may potentiate the hyperkalemia (Reubi & Vorburger, 1976).

Fluid retention may also occur, sometimes to the degree of pulmonary edema. Hemodialysis or peritoneal dialysis may be indicated with actual or potential pulmonary edema, hyperkalemic acidosis, and uremia that is uncontrolled with other interventions. Dialysis may also be indicated for other possible uremic complications (e.g., pericarditis).

Nonoliguric ATN

The patient who is nonoliguric has a better prognosis than the patient who is oliguric. The duration of the ATN may be only 5 to 8 days.

Hyperkalemia may also be a problem for such a patient. Nonoliguric ATN is associated with a decrease in tubular damage, and dialysis is needed less often.

It is important to assess the patient's state of catabolism at the onset of ATN. Catabolism results in an increased amount of tissue breakdown. Complications that increase catabolism are trauma, fever, and infections. Laboratory values will be increased (e.g., blood urea nitrogen [BUN] greater than 30 mg/dL, serum creatinine greater than 2 mg/dL). A noncatabolic patient has a BUN and creatinine that is much lower and easier to maintain (Conger & Anderson, 1983).

Medical Management of ATN

Medical management of ATN is as follows:

- correct fluid imbalances
- prevent hyperkalemia and other life-threatening electrolyte imbalances
- treat azotemic acidosis
- prevent further nephrotoxicity by altering therapy
- improve nutritional status
- prevent or treat infection
- prevent anemia

Diuresis

A diuretic phase follows oliguria (a recovery phase follows the nonoliguric phase). The patient's urine output increases. Fluid replacement is important. Fluid losses generally are replaced with the type of fluid lost. Usually 5% dextrose in one-half normal saline solution is the fluid used, and replacement is two thirds of the previous hour's urine output plus 30 mL (insensible loss). Potassium may be added if it is being lost. Diuresis usually lasts for 48 to 72 hours but may continue for as long as 7 to 12 days before normal renal function returns.

Recovery

A recovery phase follows the nonoliguric phase or the diuretic phase. Recovery may take several months to a year (Finn & Chevalier, 1979). There is a gradual return toward normal serum BUN and creatinine levels.

Postrenal ARF

Postrenal ARF is caused by any condition that results in obstruction to urine flow from the kidney to the urinary meatus. Common causes include bladder neck, urethral, and prostatic obstructions. There is a rapid reversal with surgery (an obstructive cause should always be suspected with the sudden cessation of urine output).

Three groups of patients are at high risk for obstruction:

1. children with congenital abnormalities of posterior or ureteropelvic function
2. women with cervical cancer involving the ureterovesical junction
3. elderly men with prostatic enlargement

With bilateral obstruction, the patient presents with renal failure. The patient usually complains of lower abdominal pain, and biochemical alterations may be present. The duration of the obstruction is important because the possibility of complications is increased with the length of time urine flow is impeded. Complications associated with obstruction include urinary tract infections and pyelonephritis.

Diagnosis of Obstruction

The diagnosis of obstruction is based on the patient's history, results of the physical examination and laboratory tests, and—primarily—results of the radiologic examination. The initial x-ray should be a flat plate of the abdomen, which will reveal the kidney and renal pelvis size and the patency of the urinary tract. The most common finding with an obstruction is a dilated renal pelvis. Ultrasonography will assist in revealing a dilated renal pelvis.

A urologic examination may also assist in the diagnosis. Cystoscopy will demonstrate an obstruction in the posterior urethra and bladder. A retrograde pyelogram will examine the renal collecting system. An antegrade pyelogram is used when a source of obstruction cannot be bypassed. It involves passing a catheter into the renal pelvis and removing the obstruction, if possible.

Medical Management of Obstruction

The goal of medical management is to remove the source of obstruction. It is important to stabilize and maintain the patient after removal of the obstruction. Diuresis usually occurs after removal. It is very important to measure intake and output and to record weight daily. Intravenous replacement therapy calls for two thirds of the previous hour's output plus 30 mL (insensible loss). Usually replacement is done with 5% dextrose in one-half normal saline solution. It is important to monitor electrolytes and acid-base parameters. Recovery is noted by a gradual return to normal urine output and normal serum BUN and creatinine levels.

Infection Prevention

Infection is the primary cause of death in ARF. It is essential that aseptic technique be used as indicated (e.g., for intravenous line placement). It is also important to maintain the integrity of skin and mucous membranes. Tubes and devices should be removed as soon as possible. Appropriate antibiotics should be administered after cultures are obtained.

Conclusion

It is important to recognize patients who may be at high risk for developing ARF. These include patients undergoing surgery, patients who are hemodynamically unstable, and patients receiving nephrotoxic medications or large amounts of radiologic contrast medium. Prophylactic diuresis may prevent renal damage. A solution of 5% dextrose in one-half normal saline is usually infused at a rate of 200 mL/hour for 1 hour; the rate is then decreased to 150 mL/hour. Mannitol (20 mg) may then be administered. If there is no response to the diuretic therapy (no increase in urine output) or if there is threatened fluid overload, furosemide, 40 to 80 mg intravenously, may be used to replace the mannitol. The goal of the diuresis is to promote hydration, which assists in preventing a low blood flow. The diuresis may also dilute the nephrotoxic effects of some medications.

Homeostasis should be restored as quickly as possible. Conditions that could cause complications should be avoided (e.g., fluid and electrolyte imbalances). Intake and output, central venous pressure, wedge pressure, and weight should be monitored accurately. Electrolyte imbalances must be prevented because they may be life-threatening.

Indications for dialysis in ARF are

- volume overload
- uncontrollable hyperkalemia
- uncontrollable acidosis
- symptomatic uremia
- pericarditis
- BUN levels greater than 100 mg/dL

Patients usually become symptomatic from azotemia when the BUN level is between 70 and 100 mg/dL. The desired goal is to keep the BUN in this range. The patient's clinical situation will direct the most appropriate form of dialysis. Rapid correction of uncontrollable azotemia or electrolyte imbalances (e.g., hyperkalemia) can be better managed with hemodialysis. Peritoneal dialysis may be more appropriate for patients with a limited degree of tissue breakdown.

CHRONIC RENAL FAILURE

Chronic renal failure (CRF) is a slow, progressive loss of renal function that usually occurs over a period of months to years. The result of CRF is end-stage renal failure. During CRF, regardless of the etiology, nephron damage occurs in a progressive manner, which accounts for the slow evolution of end-stage renal disease. Nondamaged nephrons compensate for the loss of functioning nephrons by doubling in size. These intact nephrons can accept larger blood volumes and perform larger clearances to compensate for the damaged nephrons. The kidney can maintain function with a nephron loss as great as 80%.

There are several causes of CRF, including glomerulonephritis, polycystic kidney disease, and obstructive nephropathy. There are four stages of chronic renal failure:

1. diminished renal reserve
2. renal insufficiency
3. end-stage renal failure
4. uremic syndrome

Diminished Renal Reserve

In diminished renal reserve, there is a 50% loss of nephron function. The remaining nephrons compensate well despite the loss. The patient is usually free of symptoms because of the kidney's ability to maintain homeostasis, preserving some excretory and regulatory functions. The serum creatinine value usually doubles but may remain in the normal range.

Renal Insufficiency

In renal insufficiency, there is a 75% loss of nephron function. This stage is manifested by mild azotemia, slightly impaired ability to concentrate urine, and anemia. The serum creatinine value quadruples, to about 5.0 mg/dL. The primary goal is to assist the patient to maintain this creatinine level. Avoiding conditions that may exacerbate existing damage assists in achieving this goal. Examples of such conditions are infection, dehydration, nephrotoxic drugs, and cardiac failure.

End-Stage Renal Failure

End-stage renal failure produces a 90% loss of nephron function. The serum creatinine value is about 10 mg/dL. At this point homeostasis can no longer be maintained, and dialysis or transplantation is necessary to maintain life.

Uremic Syndrome

Uremic syndrome, the final stage of CRF, is the systemic response of the body to the accumulation of uremic waste products. Dialysis or kidney transplantation prior to the onset of symptoms prevents this syndrome. Increasing the frequency or effectiveness of dialysis will minimize the symptoms once they appear.

Early Symptoms

Early symptoms of uremic syndrome include change in personality, increased fatigue level, malaise, nausea, and vomiting.

Symptoms associated with high levels of uremic toxins include a shortened memory span, decreased concentration time, and sleep disturbances (insomnia and nightmares).

Untreated symptoms lead to increased fatigue levels and drowsiness, which can progress to stupor, coma, and death. Uremia is often associated with psychiatric disorders, including personality changes, neuroses, and psychoses.

Physiologic Manifestations

Anemia (Skin Pallor). Anemia may be complicated by a bleeding abnormality caused by the uremia, which results from a decrease in clotting factors, an alteration in platelet aggregation, and a disorder of prothrombin consumption. Thrombocytopenia and malnutrition are other complications of anemia.

Skin Integrity. Manifestations include bruising, uncontrollable pruritus caused by urate crystal deposits (these toxins cause dryness and the appearance of a thin, white film known as uremic frost), petechiae, and ecchymoses. Skin pigments vary, producing a yellow-orange hue.

Metabolic Abnormalities. Metabolic abnormalities include carbohydrate intolerance, pseudodiabetes, and hypocalcemia secondary to the inability to convert vitamin D_3 to the active form. Hyperlipidemia may accelerate the atherosclerotic process associated with aging.

Other Manifestations

Other manifestations of uremia include the following problems.

Peripheral Neuropathies. "Restless leg syndrome" is a neurologic manifestation that begins with foot drop and burning sensations in the lower extremities. If not alleviated, peripheral neuropathy can contribute to progressive demyelinization of the distal portion of the nerves from the lower to the upper extremities, which may lead to paraplegia.

Gastrointestinal Manifestations. Stress and peptic ulcers, probably caused by the high gastrin levels associated with uremia, may develop.

Uremic Bowel. Uremic bowel is a late syndrome in which the usual state of constipation shifts to one of chronic diarrhea. Sodium polystyrene sulfonate (Kayexalate) may be ineffective in the treatment of uremic bowel.

Pericarditis. Pericarditis is a common cardiac problem manifested by symptoms of precordial pain usually associated with a pericardial friction rub. Radiologic examination reveals pleural effusion. Daily dialysis corrects this condition.

Pulmonary Manifestations. Pulmonary manifestations of uremia include pulmonary edema and uremic pneumonitis, indicated on a chest x-ray by a butterfly configuration.

ELECTROLYTE DISTURBANCES IN RENAL FAILURE

Patients with renal disease may experience numerous alterations in electrolyte balance. It is important for the nurse to recognize signs and symptoms of each electrolyte disturbance so that appropriate interventions can be carried out.

Sodium Imbalance

Sodium is the major cation of extracellular fluid. It has four major functions in the body:

1. promotes the normal distribution and volume of fluids in the body by creating and maintaining the normal osmolality of those fluids
2. enhances transcellular movement of substances by altering cell permeability
3. promotes normal neuromuscular irritability by enhancing the conduction and transmission of electrochemical impulses
4. contributes to the regulation of acid-base balance by exchanging with selected cations such as potassium and hydrogen and by combining with certain anions such as chloride and bicarbonate

The kidneys are primarily responsible for regulating sodium reabsorption and excretion. Approximately 99% of the total filtered load of sodium is reabsorbed by various parts of the nephron, leaving only about 1% to be excreted in the urine.

Hyponatremia

Hyponatremia results from either dilutional fluid expansion or a deficit of sodium. Causes of dilutional fluid expansion include excessive ingestion or infusion of electrolyte-free solutions, excessive use of tap-water enemas, irrigation of gastrointestinal tubes with electrolyte-free solutions, renal dysfunction, inappropriate secretion of antidiuretic hormone, cirrhosis, congestive heart failure, and hyperglycemia.

Sodium deficit may be caused by inadequate ingestion of dietary sodium, infusions of solutions that are sodium-deficient, salt-wasting renal dysfunction, potent diuretic therapy, adrenal insufficiency, severe vomiting, severe diarrhea, excessive perspiration, gastrointestinal suction, potassium depletion, burns, "third spacing," and severe malnutrition.

Signs and Symptoms. Signs and symptoms of hyponatremia include the following:

- serum sodium level less than 135 mEq/L
- serum chloride level less than 96 mEq/L
- variable urine sodium level, usually less than 20 mEq/L
- urine osmolality usually less than 20 mOsm/L
- urine specific gravity less than 1.010
- fatigue
- muscle weakness
- lethargy
- confusion

- headache
- tremors
- hyperreflexia
- convulsions
- coma
- apprehension
- anorexia
- nausea and vomiting
- abdominal cramps
- diarrhea
- oliguria

Treatment. Treatment of hyponatremia includes the restriction of fluid intake (if the imbalance is a result of a dilutional experience) and sometimes the administration of diuretics. Replacement therapy in the form of dietary provisions or hypertonic or isotonic saline infusions may be necessary.

Hypernatremia

Hypernatremia is caused by one of two types of conditions: (1) a condition that results in either the loss of water in excess of sodium loss or the inadequate replacement of water or (2) a condition that fosters sodium retention or excess. Examples of the first type include decreased water intake, the inability to swallow, unconsciousness, unavailability of fluids, vomiting, diarrhea, diabetes insipidus, osmotic diuresis, fever, heat stroke, high environmental temperature, hyperventilation, and dialysis therapy. Examples of the second type include excessive ingestion or infusion of sodium chloride, ingestion of sea water, acidosis, renal dysfunction, primary hyperaldosteronism, excessive use of corticosteroid therapy, and neurologic lesions.

Signs and Symptoms. Signs and symptoms of hypernatremia include the following:

- serum sodium level greater than 146 mEq/L
- serum chloride level greater than 106 mEq/L
- urine sodium level less than 50 mEq/L
- urine chloride level less than 50 mEq/L
- urine osmolality greater than 800 mOsm/L

- urine specific gravity greater than 1.030
- dry, sticky mucous membranes
- rough, dry tongue
- flushed, dry skin
- increased tissue turgor
- thirst
- decreased lacrimation
- elevated body temperature
- tachycardia
- oliguria
- lethargy
- central nervous system irritability
- muscle rigidity and weakness
- tremors
- seizures
- coma

Treatment. If the imbalance is due to a loss of extracellular fluid, intravenous saline solution should be administered to correct the imbalance. If the imbalance is due to a sodium excess, the individual's daily sodium intake should be restricted to 0.5 g to 2 g, and intravenous 5% dextrose and water should be given to replace the intracellular fluid deficit created by the hypernatremia.

Phosphorus Imbalance

Phosphorus has seven major functions in the body:

1. participates as a structural element in the bones
2. influences the production of energy sources by the red blood cells (necessary for oxygen delivery)
3. participates in the metabolism of carbohydrates, lipids, and nucleic acids
4. acts as the major urinary buffer in the formation of titratable acid
5. participates in oxidative phosphorylation
6. influences the absorption of glucose and glycerol in the intestines
7. maintains the structural integrity of the cell wall

The renal regulation of phosphorus is excretory in nature; it is dependent primarily on the serum phosphate concentration and the presence of parathyroid hormone. These two factors affect renal excretion by determining the amount and rate at which phosphate can be reabsorbed by the kidney.

Hypophosphatemia

Hypophosphatemia results from primary renal tubular defects in phosphate reabsorption, states of chronic metabolic acidosis (e.g., as in states of renal tubular acidosis), hypokalemia, extracellular fluid volume expansion, administration of phosphate binders, vomiting, malabsorption, undernutrition, prolonged use of phosphate-free intravenous solutions, abnormalities in vitamin D metabolism, alcohol withdrawal, and severe burns.

Signs and Symptoms. Signs and symptoms of hypophosphatemia include the following:

- serum phosphorus level less than 2 mg/dL
- irritability
- confusion
- disorientation
- seizures
- coma
- anisocoria (inequity in size of pupils of both eyes)
- ptosis
- nystagmus
- muscle weakness
- paresthesias
- tremors
- ataxia
- ballismus (involuntary movements)
- dysrhythmia
- hyperventilation
- anorexia
- nausea and vomiting
- bruising
- bone pain

- pathologic fractures
- arthralgias

Treatment. Replacement therapy may be implemented with either oral or intravenous phosphate preparations. In mild disturbances, dietary substances may increase the serum phosphorus level.

Hyperphosphatemia

Hyperphosphatemia is caused by renal dysfunction (most common), hypoparathyroidism, pseudohypoparathyroidism, hyperthyroidism, excessive ingestion or infusion of phosphate salts, catabolic states, neoplastic diseases, and overingestion of vitamin D metabolites.

Signs and Symptoms. Because of the inverse relationship between phosphorus and calcium in extracellular fluid, the signs and symptoms of hyperphosphatemia are the same as those of hypocalcemia. Those signs and symptoms are as follows:

- numbness and tingling of the extremities
- circumoral tingling
- muscle cramps
- tetany
- positive Chvostek's and Trousseau's signs
- epileptiform seizures
- laryngeal stridor
- carpopedal spasms
- hyperreflexia
- mental depression
- psychoses
- cardiac arrest
- abdominal cramps
- nausea and vomiting
- pathologic fractures

Treatment. Treatment for hyperphosphatemia includes restricting the intake of phosphorus; administering intestinal phosphate-binding agents, such as aluminum hydroxide gel; administering diuretics, if renal function is present; and implementing dialysis if renal dysfunction is present.

Potassium Imbalance

Potassium is an important component of muscle contraction. The ratio of intracellular K^+ to extracellular K^+ greatly affects the resting potential of skeletal and cardiac muscles. Most effects of hypokalemia and hyperkalemia are manifested as cardiac arrhythmias. The excitability, conductivity, and rhythmicity of cardiac muscles are markedly affected by changes in extracellular concentrations of K^+. The serum potassium level, corrected for acid-base disturbances, is a good measure of K^+ depletion or excess. The normal value for potassium is 3.5 to 5.0 mEq/L.

Hypokalemia

Possible causes of hypokalemia include gastrointestinal losses due to vomiting, diarrhea, ileostomy, cancer of the colon, fistulas (e.g., biliary, pancreatic, and gastrocolic), and nasogastric suctioning without replacement; use of K^+-sparing diuretics; insulin administration; aspirin therapy; ileal bladder; and metabolic alkalosis.

Signs and Symptoms. Signs and symptoms of hypokalemia include the following:

- serum K^+ level less than 3.0 mEq/L
- electrocardiographic (ECG) changes
  1. depression of ST segments
  2. flattening or inversion of T waves
  3. prolongation of PR intervals and QRS complexes
- anorexia
- muscle cramps and paresthesias
- muscle tenderness
- lethargy, apathy, drowsiness, confusion, irritability
- arrhythmias
- sinus bradycardia with first- and second-degree heart block
- atrial flutter and paroxysmal atrial tachycardia (atrioventricular dissociation and ventricular fibrillation)
- impaired renal concentrating ability and tubular degeneration with chronic hypokalemia
- predisposition to digoxin toxicity

Treatment. Hypokalemia is treated by potassium administration. The hypokalemia is corrected more easily as the normal serum K^+ level is reached. Correction should be limited to 30% to 50% in a 24-hour period.

Hyperkalemia

Hyperkalemia can be caused by acute and chronic renal failure and by metabolic acidosis.

Signs and Symptoms. Signs and symptoms of hyperkalemia include the following:

- serum K^+ level greater than 6.0 to 7.0 mEq/L
- ECG changes
  1. tenting T waves
  2. heightened T waves
  3. QRS widening
- atrial arrest
- cardiac arrest
- occasional weakness and flaccid-type paralysis

Treatment. In acute renal failure, hyperkalemia is treated by intravenous infusion of calcium (slow drip with continuous ECG monitoring, to decrease the K^+ concentration until other therapies have taken effect); infusion of sodium bicarbonate (rapid, especially if the patient is acidotic); administration of glucose and insulin (lowers K^+ by increasing glycogen deposition and therefore decreases K^+ capacity); use of exchange resins (e.g., sodium polystyrene sulfonate [Kayexalate]); and emergency dialysis.

In chronic renal failure, glucose and sodium bicarbonate are of no value because the patient usually has normal stores of glycogen and is not acidotic. The only emergency treatment is calcium infusion until dialysis can be instituted.

Calcium Imbalance

Calcium has several important functions in the body: it acts as a coenzyme in blood coagulation and plays important roles in neural transmission, smooth muscle contraction, and glycogen breakdown in striated muscle. Calcium may also act as an internal mediator in the production of some hormones. Calcium acts as an internal mediator of "second messenger" for vasoactive substances and neural innervation of cell membranes. The serum calcium level responds to two hormones: parathyroid hormone, which elevates the calcium level, and thyrocalcitonin, which lowers the calcium level. The normal serum calcium value is 4.5 to 5.5 mEq/L.

Free, nonbound calcium (dissociated) represents 55% of total body calcium content; the other 45% is bound to nondiffusible proteins or diffusible anions.

Hypocalcemia

Possible causes of hypocalcemia include chronic renal insufficiency, rickets, osteomalacia, and hypoalbuminemia. Surgical procedures during which hyperfusion has occurred may cause hypocalcemia as a result of cellular calcium shifts with sodium. A hypoactive parathyroid gland, partial or total parathyroidectomy, excessive infusion of citrated blood (calcium binds to citrate), and peritonitis may also cause hypocalcemia.

Signs and Symptoms. Signs and symptoms of hypocalcemia include the following:

- plasma calcium level less than 4.5 mEq/L
- ECG changes
  1. lengthened QT interval
  2. prolonged ST interval
- tachyarrhythmias
- tingling in fingers
- tetany with latent Chvostek's and Trousseau's signs
- muscle cramps
- convulsions

Treatment. Acute hypocalcemia is treated by administration of calcium chloride or calcium gluconate. Chronic hypocalcemia is treated by administration of a calcium salt medication.

Hypercalcemia

Possible causes of hypercalcemia include metastatic bone disease, parathyroid gland tumors, excessive vitamin D intake, and multiple myeloma.

Signs and Symptoms. Signs and symptoms of hypercalcemia include the following:

- serum calcium level greater than 5.8 mEq/L
- ECG changes
  1. shortened QT interval
  2. decreased ST segment

- flank pain
- deep thigh pain
- muscle relaxation

Treatment. Treatment of hypercalcemia includes increasing renal excretion with diuretics (e.g., furosemide) and hydration except when contraindicated by renal failure. Corticosteroid therapy should also be instituted.

Magnesium Imbalance

Magnesium acts as an important coenzyme, especially in phosphate transfers with release of energy. It also acts directly on the myoneural junction and may serve as a sympathetic blockade. Magnesium mediates neural transmission in the central nervous system and regulates skeletal muscle tension; in conjunction with adenosine triphosphate, it is active in enzyme reactions that control muscle fiber relaxation and contraction. Magnesium plays a role in glycogenesis in skeletal and cardiac fibers. The normal magnesium level is 1.5 to 2.5 mEq/L. Thirty-three percent is bound to protein. Mg^{++} is the other important intracellular cation, along with K^+.

Hypomagnesemia

Possible causes of hypomagnesemia include chronic alcoholism, prolonged vomiting or diarrhea, impaired intestinal absorption, primary hyperaldosteronism, and prolonged gastrointestinal suction or gastric outlet obstruction. Any process causing intracellular depletion, such as hypovolemic shock, can cause hypomagnesemia.

Signs and Symptoms. Signs and symptoms of hypomagnesemia include the following:

- serum magnesium level less than 1.5 mEq/L
- hyperirritability of nervous system
- involuntary movements
- coarse tremors
- positive Babinski's sign
- nystagmus
- hypertension
- flushing

Treatment. Treatment of hypomagnesemia includes intravenous infusion of magnesium chloride or magnesium sulfate, 10 to 40 mEq every 24 hours. Magnesium sulfate, 1 to 2 g every 24 hours, may be given intramuscularly.

Hypermagnesemia

Possible causes of hypermagnesemia include renal insufficiency, shock, injections of magnesium sulfate, and ingestions of large amounts of magnesium-containing laxatives and antacids.

Signs and Symptoms. Signs and symptoms of hypermagnesemia include the following:

- serum magnesium level less than 2.5 mEq/L
- ECG changes
  1. increased PR interval
  2. broadened QRS
  3. elevated T waves
- muscle weakness and paralysis
- hypotension secondary to a vasodilatory effect
- sedation and confusion

Treatment. Treatment of hypermagnesemia includes correction of renal insufficiency or shock states and institution of dialysis. Calcium may be given temporarily as an antagonist to magnesium.

CHRONIC RENAL DISEASE

It is important to determine the etiology of the patient's end-stage renal disease in order to determine his or her prognosis and therapeutic interventions. End-stage renal disease may result from a number of different disease entities. The following is a discussion of the major causes of chronic renal disease.

Glomerular Disease

Chronic glomerulonephritis is the most common form of CRF. Glomerular injury results from antigen-antibody complexes. An antibody specific to glomerular basement membrane (anti-GBM antibody) is the cause in some instances. The degree of chronic immunologic destruction is categorized as follows:

- diffuse—damage involves changes to some portion of all the glomeruli
- focal—one group of glomeruli is affected and other groups are not
- local—a specific part of the glomerulus is affected
- proliferative—glomerular mesangial or endothelial cells are affected and can affect the glomerular tuft
- membranous—changes that occur in the glomerular wall cause a thickening secondary to an immunologic reaction
- necrotizing—fibroid is deposited in the glomerulus
- sclerotic—glomerular scarring from a prior injury is present

A diagnosis of glomerulonephritis is made by identifying the presence of one or more of the deposited immune complexes. The immunoglobulins (IgG, IgA, IgM), complement (C_3, C_4), and fibrin are immune complexes that have important diagnostic implications. Damage to the glomerulus by the various immunologic tissue reactions causes cellular proliferation, leukocyte infiltration, basement membrane thickening, and sclerosis (Leaf & Cotran, 1985). Phagocytosis and enzyme release occur in the area of the immune response.

Electron and immunofluorescent microscopy are used in determining the type of glomerulonephropathy present. Electron microscopy may reveal morphologic changes in the glomerular capillary wall. Immunofluorescence displays the components of the immunologic system involved in the glomerular reaction. Percutaneous renal biopsy may also be done.

Patients with glomerulonephritis may present with no symptoms or may present with hypertension or abnormalities in the urine, such as proteinuria or hematuria.

Hypertensive Disease

Hypertensive disease causes a rapid acceleration of the atherosclerotic process usually associated with aging. Decreased perfusion, tissue infarction, and ischemic injury to target organs (kidney, heart, brain) result from arteriolar narrowing and possible occlusion. Hypertension causes renal damage. Progressive hypertensive disease may cause diffusive thickening of the afferent arterioles. Nephrosclerotic changes progress to create an ischemic state that damages both glomeruli and tubules. Renal arterioles are damaged even more by severe uncontrolled or malignant hypertension. This type of renal damage results in end-stage renal failure.

Urinary Tract Infection

Uremia causes immunosuppression in patients with renal failure, which is the primary reason for an increased susceptibility to urinary tract infection (UTI) in these patients.

UTI of bacterial origin is the most common infection. Fungi and parasitic organisms also cause UTI. The exact location of the UTI may vary from the kidney to the urethra. A fecal contaminant such as *Escherichia coli* is usually the invading organism. Bladder catheterization, urinary stasis secondary to obstruction, reflux of urine, and immunosuppression are factors that may contribute to the development of UTI. Other causes of UTI include sexual intercourse, advancing age (over age 60 years) in women, and prostatic disease in men.

UTI is usually diagnosed by culture of the urine. Minimizing contamination is very important when the urine specimen is obtained for culture. A colony count of more than 10^5/mL in a voided specimen is indicative of UTI.

Symptoms of bladder infection include dysuria, frequency, and pain in the suprapubic region. These symptoms differ from those of kidney infection, which are flank pain, nausea, vomiting, and microscopic hematuria.

Chronic Pyelonephritis

A history of infected renal stones, hematuria, flank pain, or vesicourethral reflux, especially in conjunction with persistent infections, assists in the diagnosis of chronic pyelonephritis.

Urine cultures positive for pyuria and occasional white cell casts may also indicate chronic pyelonephritis. A positive urine culture is not required for diagnosis. An intravenous pyelogram reveals small kidneys, cortical scarring, and dilated or blunted calices.

Renal Cancers

Renal and urinary carcinomas can be another cause of chronic renal failure. Initially the tumor is limited to a specific area of the urinary tract or to the kidney, but it commonly—within a short time after onset—metastasizes to other sites. Approximately 1 billion cells must be present before the cancer can be detected clinically. A tumor containing more than 5 billion cells is associated with systemic involvement and a poor prognosis.

Benign renal tumors include adenoma, hemangiopericytoma, hemangioma, and hematoma. Renal carcinomas include nephroblastoma, adenocarcinoma, renal cell carcinoma, and sarcoma. Renal cancers develop more often in men with a higher incidence between ages 50 and 60 years. Cigarette smoking is believed to be the major risk factor in renal carcinoma.

An intravenous pyelogram is indicated in diagnosing renal carcinoma. Distortions in the outline of the kidney are suggestive of a renal mass. A solid mass may be distinguished from a cystic tumor by ultrasonography or computed tomography. Renal masses may be distinguished with nuclear magnetic resonance. Tumors can be located and staged by angioplasty.

Tubulointerstitial Disease

Tubulointerstitial disease represents a group of renal disorders affecting the tubular or interstitial regions of the kidney, or both. The causes of these disorders are metabolic imbalances, mechanical alterations, immunologic disorders, and hereditary diseases.

Diagnosis of tubulointerstitial disease should include a history assessment for drug usage, exposure to nephrotoxic agents, or frequent urinary tract infections. Urine cultures, serum electrolytes, and urinalysis may assist in the diagnosis. Renal biopsy may be necessary if no direct cause can be determined from the above information.

REFERENCES

Burke, T.J., & Schrier, R.W. (1983). Ischemic acute renal failure: Pathogenic steps leading to acute tubular necrosis. *Circulatory Shock, 11*, 245–253.

Conger, J.D. (1983). Vascular abnormalities in the maintenance of acute renal failure. *Circulatory Shock, 11*, 235–244.

Conger, J.D., & Anderson, R.J. (1983). Acute renal failure including cortical necrosis. In S.G. Massry & R.J. Glasscock (Eds.), *Textbook of nephrology* (Vol. 2, pp. 6.226–6.227). Baltimore: Williams & Wilkins.

Finn, W.J., & Chevalier, R.L. (1979). Recovery from post-ischemic acute renal failure in the rat. *Kidney International, 16*, 113–123.

Goldstein, M.B. (1983). Acute renal failure. *Medical Clinics of North America, 67*(6), 1325–1341.

Hsu, C.H., & Kurtz, T.W. (1981). Renal hemodynamics in experimental acute renal failure. *Nephron, 27*, 255–259.

Kon, V., & Ichikawa, T.W. (1984). Research seminar: Physiology of acute renal failure. *Journal of Pediatrics, 105*(3), 351–357.

Leaf, A., & Cotran, R.S. (1985). *Renal pathophysiology* (3rd ed.). New York: Oxford.

Maher, J.F. (1981). Pathophysiology of renal hemodynamics. *Nephron, 27*, 215–221.

Mars, D.R., & Treloar, D. (1984). Acute tubular necrosis: Pathophysiology and treatment. *Heart & Lung, 13*(2), 194–201.

Reubi, F.C., & Vorburger, C. (1976). Renal hemodynamics in acute renal failure after shock in man. *Kidney International, 10*, 5137–5147.

Stark, J. (1985). The renal system. In J. Alspach & S. Williams (Eds.), *Core curriculum for critical care nursing*. Philadelphia: Saunders.

Stark, J. (1988). Acute renal failure. In M.R. Kinney, D.R. Packa, & S.B. Dunbar (Eds.), *AACN's clinical reference for critical care nursing* (2nd ed.). New York: McGraw-Hill.

Wilson, M.F., & Brackett, D.J. (1983). Release of vasoactive hormones and circulatory changes in shock. *Circulatory Shock, 11*, 225–234.

SUGGESTED READINGS

Hekelman, F.P., & Ostendarp, C.A. (1979). *Nephrology nursing perspectives of care*. New York: McGraw-Hill.

Lancaster, L.E. (1987). Manifestations of renal failure. In L.E. Lancaster (Ed.), *Core curriculum for nephrology nursing*. Pitman, NJ: American Nephrology Nurses' Association.

Schoengrund, L., & Balzer, P. (Eds.). (1985). *Renal problems in critical care*. New York: Wiley.

Stark, J.L. (1988). Acute renal failure. In M.R. Kinney, D.R. Packa, & S.B. Dunbar (Eds.), *AACN's clinical reference for critical care nursing* (2nd ed.). New York: McGraw-Hill.

Stark, J.L., & Kelleher, R. (1988). Chronic renal failure. In M.R. Kinney, D.R. Packa, & S.B. Dunbar (Eds.), *AACN's clinical reference for critical care nursing* (2nd ed.). New York: McGraw-Hill.

5

Hemodialysis

One form of treatment for end-stage renal disease is hemodialysis. Hemodialysis partially replaces the excretory functions of the kidney, but it does not replace the hormonal functions. The elimination of wastes, excess electrolytes, and water is accomplished by the processes of diffusion and ultrafiltration.

Patients may have the option of choosing to undergo hemodialysis at home or in-center. Some patients may have the option of self-dialysis at an in-center facility whereby a nurse assists in monitoring them during their treatment. Regional availability has to be considered initially in the selection of which form of hemodialysis is best for the patient. Other factors that determine which method of hemodialysis is best are the patient's physical condition and the availability of family or significant others for the assistance needed in home hemodialysis.

PATIENT SELECTION FOR MAINTENANCE DIALYSIS

Patient selection for maintenance dialysis is determined by

- creatinine clearance less than 10 mL/min
- elevated serum creatinine level
- evidence of uremia
- presence or absence of other chronic or incapacitating illness
- expectation of reasonable rehabilitation
- patient desire

BASIC CONCEPTS RELATED TO SOLUTE REMOVAL

Diffusion

Diffusion is the movement of a molecule from a region of higher concentration to a region of lower concentration. The difference in the region of concentration that causes movement of molecules is called a concentration gradient.

Factors that affect the rate of diffusion in hemodialysis are

- molecule size (molecules too large to pass through the pores in the semipermeable membrane are nondiffusible)
- size and number of pores in the semipermeable membrane
- surface area of the semipermeable membrane (the larger the surface area, the more rapidly diffusion occurs)
- temperature of the solutions on either side of the semipermeable membrane (the higher the temperature of the solutions, the more rapidly diffusion occurs)
- concentration of solutes in the blood (the higher the concentration gradient for a given solute, the more rapidly diffusion occurs; when equilibrium of a solute occurs on both sides of the membrane, diffusion ceases)
- thickness of the semipermeable membrane
- resistance to flow caused by blood film layer, dialyzing fluid film layer, the membrane, or dialyzer configuration
- solute drag (solutes cross the semipermeable membrane with water)

Clearance

Clearance expresses the performance of the dialyzing process. It is the amount of solute removed from the blood as it flows through the dialyzer or the volume of blood totally cleared of a solute by the dialyzer in 1 minute. Clearance deals with the solute concentration in blood and does not consider the solute concentration in the dialysate. Dialysate solute concentration may affect the clearance of solutes.

BASIC CONCEPTS RELATED TO WATER REMOVAL

Ultrafiltration

Ultrafiltration is the rate of fluid removed under pressure, measured in milliliters per minute. Fluid removal has two components, that due to osmotic pressure and that due to hydrostatic pressure.

Osmotic Pressure

Osmosis is the passage of a solvent (water) across a semipermeable membrane from an area of lesser solute concentration to an area of greater solute concentration; the force that causes the water to move through the membrane is called osmotic pressure.

In dialysis, glucose in excess of blood glucose levels is added to the dialysate to cause an osmotic gradient between blood and dialysate (more frequently in peritoneal dialysis); the net effect is that water moves from the plasma into the dialysate as long as the osmotic gradient exists. Ultrafiltration caused by osmosis is difficult to measure and is unpredictable.

Hydrostatic Pressure

Hydrostatic pressure is the pressure that a liquid exerts against the wall of its container. In hemodialysis, pressures are applied to blood and dialysate compartments to accomplish ultrafiltration in the blood compartment; a positive pressure is applied to push water from the plasma across the semipermeable membrane; in the dialysate compartment, a negative pressure is applied to pull water from the blood compartment across the semipermeable membrane. The net sum of the two pressures is the transmembrane pressure.

COMPONENTS OF A HEMODIALYSIS SYSTEM

Circulatory Access

A high-blood-flow vascular access is required in order to perform hemodialysis. There are various types of vascular accesses, which are described in detail later in this chapter.

Blood Pump

The function of the blood pump is to assist the heart in propelling blood through the tubing and the dialyzer (extracorporeal circuit). The blood pump operates by having two or more rollers rotate in a closed compartment; the blood tubing is squeezed against a semicircular wall; the roller is calibrated to give a proper rate of blood flow (Figure 5-1).

Dialyzers

Three types of dialyzers are the coil, the parallel plate, and the hollow fiber dialyzers (Figures 5-2, 5-3, and 5-4). All three types have the follow-

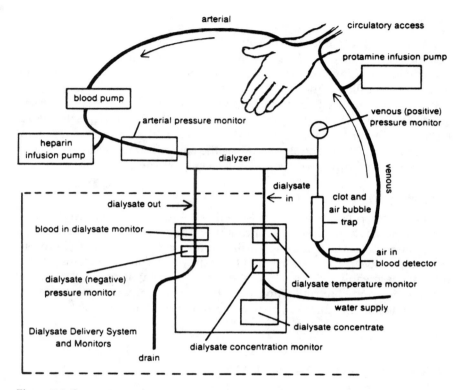

Figure 5-1 Components of a typical hemodialysis system. *Source:* From *Core Curriculum for Nephrology Nursing* (p. 191) by L.E. Lancaster, 1987, Pitman, NJ: American Nephrology Nurses' Association. Copyright 1987 by American Nephrology Nurses' Association. Reprinted by permission.

ing characteristics in common: Blood and dialysate are pumped on opposite sides of a semipermeable membrane contained in a closed compartment. The blood contains excess quantities of specific solutes (metabolic waste products and electrolytes). The dialysate is free of metabolic waste products and has a lower concentration of electrolytes than does the blood. Because of the concentration gradient, excess metabolic waste products diffuse across the semipermeable membrane from blood to dialysate; electrolytes move in both directions; diffusion continues until equilibrium occurs. Red blood cells, white blood cells, and proteins are too large to diffuse across the semipermeable membrane. Water moves from the blood to the dialysate compartment by osmotic and hydrostatic pressure.

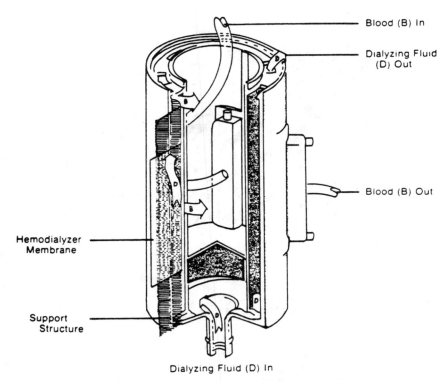

Blood (B) In

Dialyzing Fluid (D) Out

Blood (B) Out

Hemodialyzer Membrane

Support Structure

Dialyzing Fluid (D) In

Figure 5-2 Coil hemodialyzer. *Source:* From *Protecting the Future of Quality Care Through an Understanding of Hemodialysis Principles* (p. 192) by G.S. Wick and J. Parker, 1984, Pitman, NJ: American Nephrology Nurses' Association. Copyright 1984 by American Nephrology Nurses' Association. Reprinted by permission.

Anticoagulation

When blood comes in contact with foreign surfaces, such as the blood lines and the dialyzer, it tends to clot; heparin is used to prevent this tendency.

Methods of Heparin Administration

Continuous heparinization is achieved by infusing heparin throughout dialysis with a calibrated infusion pump into the arterial blood line of the dialyzer.

Intermittent heparinization is achieved by administering a loading dose of heparin at the beginning of dialysis and administering additional doses throughout the procedure.

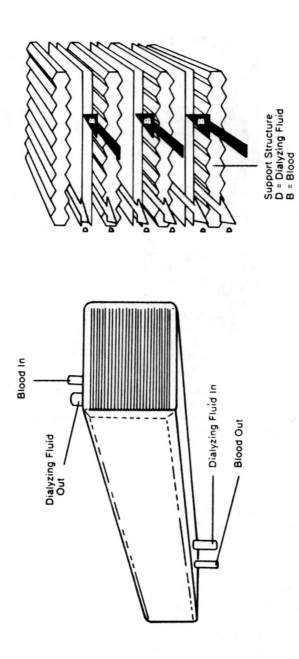

Figure 5-3 Parallel plate hemodialyzer. *Source:* From *Protecting the Future of Quality Care Through an Understanding of Hemodialysis Principles* (p. 193) by G.S. Wick and J. Parker, 1984, Pitman, NJ: American Nephrology Nurses' Association. Copyright 1984 by American Nephrology Nurses' Association. Reprinted by permission.

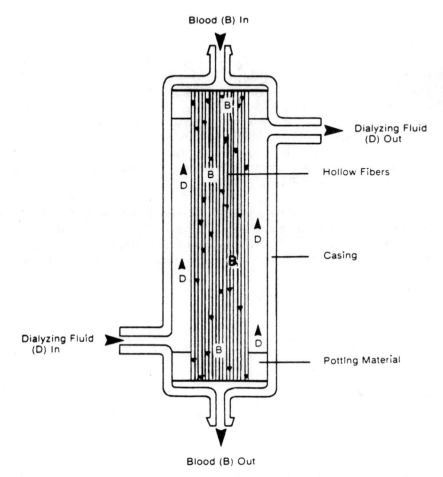

Figure 5-4 Hollow fiber hemodialyzer. *Source:* From *Protecting the Future of Quality Care Through an Understanding of Hemodialysis Principles* (p. 194) by G.S. Wick and J. Parker, 1984, Pitman, NJ: American Nephrology Nurses' Association. Copyright 1984 by American Nephrology Nurses' Association. Reprinted by permission.

Types of Heparinization

There are several types of heparinization.

Systemic Heparinization. Heparin is administered into the arterial blood line to maintain the clotting time of blood in the dialyzer at approximately two times the baseline.

Regional Heparinization. Regional heparinization is indicated for patients who have had recent surgery, who have a tendency to bleed, or who have pericarditis. Heparin is infused continuously via an infusion pump into the arterial blood line; concomitantly, protamine sulfate is infused into the venous line as blood is being returned to the patient; heparin is neutralized before blood re-enters the body, so that the patient's clotting time is maintained close to normal.

Heparin rebound may occur when large doses of heparin and protamine are used. It is caused by a breakdown of the heparin-protamine complex in the reticuloendothelial system; several hours after hemodialysis, heparin then re-enters the systemic circulation, resulting in an excess of heparin and bleeding diathesis.

Tight Heparinization. Heparin is administered according to frequently determined clotting times in order to heparinize the dialyzer sufficiently to prevent clotting (clotting time of the dialyzer is maintained at 1.25 to 1.5 times the baseline), while at the same time minimizing the heparin dose the patient receives.

Dialysate Fluid Composition

Sodium

Sodium is the major cation of the dialysate. The concentration used at various facilities ranges from 130 to 155 mEq/L (usually 135 to 140 mEq/L). Low-sodium dialysate decreases extracellular osmolality, causing a fluid shift into the cells. Higher-sodium dialysate increases extracellular osmolality and causes a shift of water out of the cells. Ideally, the sodium concentration in the dialysate should be adjusted to remove water and sodium during dialysis in amounts equal to that gained since the previous dialysis. The sodium concentration will vary depending on the patient's fluid and sodium intake.

Potassium

The potassium concentration in the dialysate ranges from 0 to 5 mEq/L, depending on the need to decrease the patient's serum potassium level. Low-potassium dialysates can precipitate cardiac arrhythmias, especially in a patient receiving a digitalis preparation. The rate at which potassium is removed during dialysis is more likely to cause arrhythmias than the amount removed.

Magnesium

The magnesium concentration may range from 0 to 3 mEq/L and is largely a matter of personal choice. It is often eliminated in patients receiving magnesium-containing phosphate binders to reduce the potential for hypermagnesemia.

Calcium

Calcium is present in plasma in protein-bound and ionized forms and as calcium complexes; ionized calcium is the physiologically important form. Decreased gastrointestinal absorption causes negative calcium balance in many patients with chronic renal failure; thus, a positive flux of calcium from the dialysate into the patient during dialysis is desirable and is dependent on the difference between dialysate calcium and ultrafilterable calcium concentration in plasma. Ultrafilterable calcium (ionized calcium and calcium complexes) equals 50% to 60% of total plasma calcium and usually averages 2.5 to 3.0 mEq/L. A dialysate concentration of 3.0 to 3.5 mEq/L (6.0 to 7.0 mg/dL) will result in a net flux of calcium into the patient from the dialysate. In patients with persistent hypocalcemia, the dialysate concentration may be increased to 4.0 to 4.5 mEq/L. High-calcium dialysate should be used with caution in patients with serum phosphate levels greater than 5.0 mg/dL because of the risk of soft tissue and vascular calcification.

Chloride

Chloride is present in the dialysate as a complex of calcium, sodium, and potassium, and the concentration will vary as those electrolyte concentrations in the dialysate change. The level should be adjusted to the physiologic norm, approximately 95 to 105 mEq/L.

Glucose

Glucose may or may not be present in the dialysate. Patients can lose 20 to 30 g of glucose during a 4-hour dialysis; thus patients who initiate dialysis without having eaten recently can become hypoglycemic and have symptoms of hypotension, nausea, and vomiting. Diabetic patients may lose even more glucose across the dialysis membrane, and may benefit from the addition of glucose (200 mg/dL) to the dialysate to prevent symptoms.

Buffers

The two most commonly used buffers for hemodialysis are acetate (usual dialysate concentration 35 to 40 mEq/L) and bicarbonate (usual dialysate concentration 36 to 39 mEq/L); either one improves acidosis; the buffer diffuses into the blood during hemodialysis. Acetate is metabolized in the liver to bicarbonate; if not readily metabolized by the liver, acetate causes myocardial depression and vasodilation, which contribute to hypotension; it also can cause headache, nausea, and vomiting. Bicarbonate does not have the side effects of acetate and is the buffer of choice for patients who have liver impairment, cardiovascular instability, lactic acidosis, or severe acid-base imbalance; patients seem to tolerate ultrafiltration with less hypotension, nausea, vomiting, and cramps.

Water Treatment

Water used for dialysis is treated to ensure that it is sufficiently pure (free of contaminants) to meet the maximal allowable levels recommended by the Association for the Advancement of Medical Instrumentation. Water used to prepare the dialysate should have a total viable microbial count not exceeding 200/mL. Product water should be cultured monthly.

MONITORING SYSTEMS OF HEMODIALYSIS MACHINES

It is important to observe the patient and the hemodialysis machine throughout dialysis in addition to the electronic monitors. The different monitors on the hemodialysis machine include

- an arterial pressure monitor, which measures the pressure of blood in the drip chamber between the patient and the dialyzer inlet
- a venous pressure monitor, which measures the pressure of blood in the drip chamber between the dialyzer outlet and the patient
- an air detector, which detects air bubbles and foam in the venous blood line by means of a photoelectric cell or ultrasound
- a conductivity monitor, which measures the electrical conductivity or concentration of dialysate
- a dialysate flow rate monitor, which measures the flow rate of dialysate
- a dialysate temperature monitor, which measures the temperature of the dialysate
- a monitor to detect blood in the dialysate
- a negative pressure monitor of the dialysate compartment

PREDIALYSIS ASSESSMENT

Predialysis assessment of the patient should be done and the following findings noted:

- predialysis weight (compare with weight from end of previous dialysis and patient's dry weight)
- blood pressure and changes from previous dialysis
- temperature
- change in mentation, speech, or thought processes
- peripheral pulses
- heart rate, rhythm, and presence of pericardial friction rub or other abnormalities
- respiratory rate, rhythm, and quality
- presence of rales or crackles in breath sounds
- skin changes
- edema

History of headache, nausea, vomiting, respiratory distress, angina, weakness, fever, or other problems the patient may have experienced since the last dialysis should be recorded. Laboratory data should be checked for serum albumin, creatinine, nitrogen, and electrolyte levels and acid-base status.

MONITORING DURING DIALYSIS

The following should be monitored during dialysis: vital signs, weight, clotting times, response to treatment, and symptoms manifested.

POSTDIALYSIS ASSESSMENT

Postdialysis assessment of the patient should include vital signs and weight compared with predialysis findings. Weight and blood pressure would be expected to be lower because of fluid removal.

CIRCULATORY ACCESS FOR HEMODIALYSIS

Standard External Arteriovenous Shunt

An external arteriovenous (AV) shunt consists of two rigid Teflon tips (or modified tip construction) implanted in an artery and a vein. Silastic tubing is attached to the Teflon vessel tip and brought to the outside through puncture wounds in the skin. The Silastic tubes are connected to allow for uninterrupted blood flow.

Indications

An external AV shunt is indicated for patients with acute or reversible renal failure, patients awaiting an immediate elective renal transplant, patients who need hemodialysis immediately, and patients awaiting maturation of an internal AV fistula.

Advantages

The advantages of the external AV shunt are that it can be used immediately after placement and requires no venipuncture.

Disadvantages

The disadvantages of the external AV shunt are a short life span due to high incidence of complications, infections, mechanical complications, frequent clotting, failure due to internal proliferation or structural defects, and day-to-day disability and alterations in body image caused by attachment to an external device.

Other Types of External AV Shunts

Various types of external AV shunts (Figure 5-5) are described below.

Scribner Shunt

The Scribner shunt consists of Teflon tips inserted into the vessels; the remainder of the shunt is constructed of Silastic tubing, which has a reverse curve so that the external portion of the shunt is directed away from the joint of the extremity.

Advantages. The advantages are that the shunt is available for immediate use and permits freedom of movement in the adjacent joint.

Disadvantages. The disadvantages are that it is difficult, if not impossible, to declot the shunt, and there is a higher incidence of thrombosis than with other types of AV shunts.

Ramirez Shunt

The Ramirez shunt is a straight cannula shunt with Silastic wings added to the embedded portion to provide stability and avoid dislodgment. It is easier to declot when thrombosis occurs.

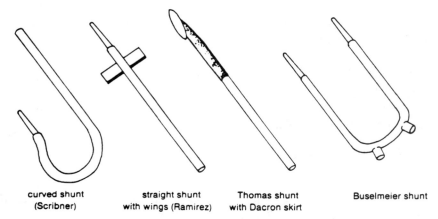

curved shunt   straight shunt   Thomas shunt   Buselmeier shunt
(Scribner)   with wings (Ramirez)   with Dacron skirt

Figure 5-5 Various types of external AV shunts. *Source:* From *Core Curriculum for Nephrology Nursing* (p. 230) by L.E. Lancaster, 1987, Pitman, NJ: American Nephrology Nurses' Association. Copyright 1987 by American Nephrology Nurses' Association. Reprinted by permission.

Buselmeier Shunt

In the Buselmeier shunt, Teflon tips are inserted into vessels in the same manner as in the standard AV shunt. The outer portion of the cannula is U-shaped with two short branches coming off each side of the curve; most of the device is subcutaneous. The obturator kept in the branches is removed for connection to blood lines to begin hemodialysis.

Advantages. The advantages are high blood flow rates, less chance for accidental dislodgment and intimal injury, and avoidance of excessive suction on the arterial wall due to built-in recirculation.

Disadvantage. The disadvantage is that septic episodes have been traced to the plugged portion of the shunt.

Thomas Shunt

The Thomas shunt consists of a face plate made of Dacron fabric attached to Silastic tubing via a Dacron sleeve.

Advantages. The advantages are an unimpeded flow to the distal extremities, small incidence of thrombosis because of high blood flow rate, and a lack of vessel stenosis because of the technique for insertion.

Disadvantages. The disadvantages include infection and sepsis, and pseudoaneurysm formation complicated by hemorrhage. The shunt is used only in patients who have no other circulatory access site.

Allen-Brown Shunt

The Allen-Brown shunt is made of an accordion-pleated sleeve of knitted Dacron to which a Silastic tube is glued; an end-to-end anastomosis is made between the vessel and the Dacron sleeve.

Advantage. The shunt can be anastomosed onto short segments of vessels.

Disadvantages. The disadvantages are similar to those of the standard external AV shunt and the Thomas shunt.

The choice of placement site depends on the type of renal failure (acute or chronic) and the availability of undamaged vessels of the proper size. The nondominant upper extremity is the preferred site for patients with reversible acute renal failure. Ankle shunts are usually used for patients whose dialysis will be long-term, thus saving the vessels in the arm for an AV fistula.

Complications of External AV Shunts

Infection. Infection is almost inevitable. Usually it is only localized cellulitis, but septicemia can occur. Prevention of infection requires meticulous daily care and avoidance of trauma when handling the shunt.

Skin Erosion. Skin erosion occurs more commonly in very thin or malnourished patients; it can lead to thrombosis.

Dislodgment/Disconnection. Dislodgment/disconnection may be a life-threatening complication that may be accidental or purposeful (suicide attempt). Dislodgment/disconnection can be prevented by covering the entire shunt with a dressing; infections at the vessel tip should be treated early.

Thrombosis. Thrombosis is the most common complication of an external AV shunt. Causes of thrombosis include malalignment of cannula tips within the vessel; bending of the vessel wall; arterial narrowing close to the cannula tip; recent thrombi; fibrosis at the cannula tip; inadequate anticoagulation; extrinsic pressure by tight bandage, jewelry, or garment; hypotension; and bending of the shunt connector.

Aspiration of the clot may be attempted, or an embolectomy may be performed by qualified personnel. Complications of an embolectomy include systemic emboli, rupture of the vessel by the catheter tip, and dislodgment of the shunt tip from the vessel.

General Care and Patient Education

Daily shunt care should include the following steps:

1. Remove dressing carefully from the shunt. Pour peroxide over the dressing until easy removal is possible if dried blood has caused the dressing to adhere to the skin.
2. Place a sterile towel under the shunt extremity.
3. Pour peroxide over the cannula insertion sites and around the shunt area. Clean the area around the shunt insertion sites with a gauze sponge to remove dried blood. Cleanse each cannula insertion site gently, using a sterile cotton-tipped applicator. Clean underneath the cannula carefully. Use a separate applicator for each side, and clean from insertion site outward.
4. Repeat step 3, using a povidone-iodine solution.
5. Apply a small amount of povidone-iodine ointment around each cannula insertion site if signs of infection are noted.
6. Place one sterile gauze sponge under the shunt and one sterile gauze sponge over the shunt.
7. Apply a gauze bandage securely around the shunt. Avoid constrictive dressing. Tape the dressing in place.
8. Place bulldog clamps on the edge of the gauze bandage so that they are readily available.
9. Keep the area clean and dry at all times; change dressing if soiled or wet.
10. Avoid extremes of heat or cold to the shunted extremity, as they predispose to clotting.
11. Avoid constrictions of the extremity above or over the shunt.
12. Prevent the patient from crossing legs if the shunt is in a leg.
13. Avoid blood pressure measurements and venipunctures in the shunted limb.
14. Teach the patient to assess the shunt for patency by observing blood in the shunt for obvious clotting and palpating with fingertips for a thrill above the venous side of a shunt.
15. Teach the patient to assess for signs of infection.

16. Teach the patient how to manage accidental separation or dislodgment.

Internal AV Fistula

An internal AV fistula is the surgical creation of an anastomosis between an artery and a vein, thus allowing arterial blood flow through the vein, causing venous engorgement and enlargement. Large-bore needles are inserted into the vein to remove and return blood for hemodialysis.

An internal AV fistula is indicated in chronic renal failure and for maintenance hemodialysis.

Advantages

The advantages of an internal AV fistula are that the patient's own vessels are preferable to synthetic devices or long-term hemodialysis. An external AV fistula lasts longer than an external AV shunt, with decreased clotting and infection rates compared with those with an external AV shunt; and there is no problem of accidental dislodgment.

Disadvantages

The disadvantages of an internal AV fistula are the length of time required for maturation before the fistula can be used for hemodialysis, and two somewhat painful needle sticks are required to initiate hemodialysis.

Types of AV Fistulas

Types of AV fistulas include (1) side-artery to side-vein anastomosis with distal vessels left open, (2) side-artery to side-vein anastomosis with distal vessels ligated, (3) end-artery to end-vein anastomosis, (4) end-vein to side-artery anastomosis, and (5) side-vein to end-artery anastomosis (Figure 5-6).

An AV fistula can be placed in either forearm, but the nondominant arm is preferred to allow the patient more freedom while on hemodialysis. The radial artery and cephalic vein or brachial artery and cephalic vein are commonly used.

Time of placement is critical. In a patient followed for progressive renal failure, the AV fistula is created when the creatinine clearance is about 15 mL/min. In patients with rapidly progressive renal failure, the AV fistula should be placed when the creatinine clearance is approximately 25 mL/min.

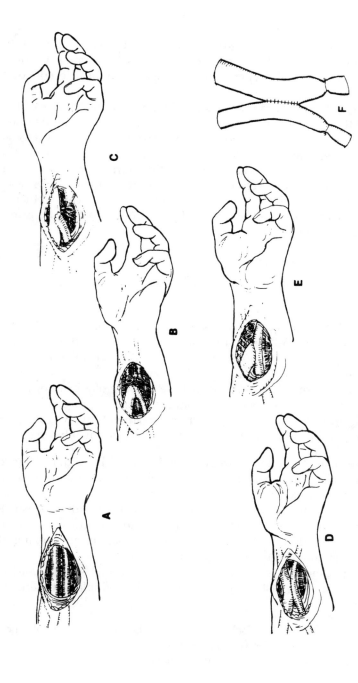

Figure 5-6 Types of internal AV fistulas. **(A)** Normal artery-vein relationship; **(B)** end-to-end anastomosis; **(C)** end-vein to side-artery anastomosis; **(D)** side-to-side anastomosis; **(E)** side-vein to end-artery anastomosis; **(F)** side-to-side converted to end-to-end anastomosis. *Source:* From *Core Curriculum for Nephrology Nursing* (p. 232) by L.E. Lancaster (Ed.). 1987, Pitman, NJ: American Nephrology Nurses' Association. Copyright 1987 by American Nephrology Nurses' Association. Reprinted by permission.

Maturation of the AV Fistula

Usually 1 to 3 months are required for the vein to mature enough to accept repeated venipunctures for hemodialysis. The veins become arterialized, and their walls hypertrophy in response to the arterial blood flow.

Maturation of the fistula can be hastened by performing exercises 10 to 14 days after the operative procedure. Initially the exercises can be done for 5 to 10 minutes four or five times per day, as follows: (1) Apply a tourniquet to the upper arm to impede venous flow and distend forearm vessels; use care not to occlude blood flow with the tourniquet, but apply it tightly enough to distend vessels. (2) Instruct the patient to open and close the fist to pump arterial blood against the venous resistance caused by the tourniquet; have the patient squeeze a rubber ball, tennis ball, hand grips, or a rolled-up sock to help exert pressure.

Complications of the AV Fistula

Complications that may occur with the use of an AV fistula are described below.

Thrombosis. Thrombosis can be caused by extrinsic pressure, as from a tight bandage or from positioning the patient so as to cause pressure over the fistula, hypovolemia or marked hypotension, or turbulence at the anastomosis site.

Signs and symptoms of thrombosis include absence of a bruit or thrill, and poor blood flow or no blood flow from the fistula.

Thrombosis is diagnosed by a fistulogram. Treatment involves surgical declotting, if possible; usually, however, another access must be created.

Venous Hypertension. Venous hypertension is caused by high resistance to flow in the proximal portion of the vein, or by any event that causes a predominantly distal flow.

Signs and symptoms include edema of the entire hand with varicosities and ulcerations, and most often a "sore thumb" syndrome consisting of an edematous cyanotic thumb with eczematous skin changes and oozing of serosanguineous fluid around the nail bed.

Venous hypertension is diagnosed by angiographic studies and is treated by ligation of the distal portion of vein or by angioplasty to remove stenotic areas.

Ischemia ("Steal Syndrome"). Ischemia results when the limb supplied by antegrade flow is deprived by retrograde flow or when short-circuiting to an area of lower resistance occurs in that artery.

Signs and symptoms include cold, painful fingers; the condition can progress to gangrene in serious cases.

Treatment of ischemia includes ligation of the distal portion of the artery, thus redirecting the retrograde flow; if collateral circulation is inadequate, the fistula is sacrificed by ligating both proximal and distal portions of the vein used to create the fistula.

Aneurysms. Aneurysms are usually a result of repeated needle punctures at the same site. Pseudoaneurysms result from hematoma formation at a puncture site.

Signs and symptoms of aneurysms are pain and reduced blood flow. Complications include the formation of thrombi and the risk of rupture.

Aneurysms are treated by surgical repair.

Infection. Infection can be localized or systemic. It is caused by a break in aseptic technique during needle insertion.

Signs and symptoms include redness, pain, swelling along the fistula site, fever, and positive blood cultures if the infection is systemic.

Antibiotic therapy is the treatment of choice.

General Care and Patient Education

General care and patient education should include the following:

1. Assess patency by palpating for a thrill over the fistula several times a day; report any changes to the primary physician.
2. Instruct the patient to avoid wearing constrictive clothing or an elastic watchband on the extremity with the fistula.
3. Instruct the patient to avoid carrying heavy objects across or above the fistula.
4. Report any signs and symptoms of inflammation or infection of fistula.
5. Avoid blood pressure measurements and venipunctures in the access limb.

AV Fistula Graft

An AV fistula graft is a biologic, semibiologic, or prosthetic graft that can be implanted subcutaneously and interposed between an artery and a vein. Needles are inserted into the graft to remove and return blood during hemodialysis.

An AV fistula graft is indicated for use in patients who have inadequate vessels or who have nutritional problems, severe obesity, marked cachexia, or self-inflicted vein loss.

Advantages

An AV fistula graft can be used sooner than a regular AV fistula. The needle puncture is usually easier to accomplish, and size and blood flow are not dependent on vein maturation.

Disadvantage

The high number of complications provides a major disadvantage.

Types of Grafts

The types of grafts available are as follows: (1) autogenous or saphenous vein graft; (2) modified human umbilical vein treated to destroy collagen cells and then covered by Dacron mesh; (3) bovine heterograft (bovine carotid artery treated to remove protein material); (4) polytetrafluoroethylene (PTFE) graft (e.g., Impra, Gore-Tex); and (5) PTFE graft with transcutaneous device for needle-free access to the circulation (e.g., Hemasite), which consists of a metal body, a self-sealing system, and a locking ring (Figure 5-7).

Advantages. The advantages are ease in initiating and discontinuing the dialysis procedure, minimal blood loss with each use, ability to declot through the device, and easy monitoring of blood flow through the device.

Disadvantages. The disadvantages are the same as in other graft-type accesses. Infections and thrombosis are major complications, and placement is expensive as it is interposed between any suitable artery and vein and placed in a subcutaneous location. The ideal placement site is the upper extremity, preferably the forearm; grafts implanted in the thigh introduce a greater risk for ischemia and infection. A straight graft versus a loop graft depends on the availability of vessels.

Complications of AV Fistula Grafts

Infection. Infection is more serious in AV fistula grafts than in AV fistulas because of the risk of disintegration and subsequent hemorrhage. Early

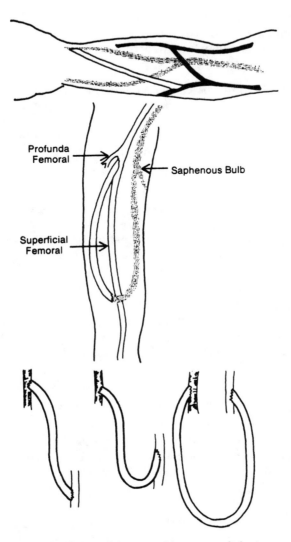

Figure 5-7 AV fistula grafts. Top, graft interposed between radial artery and basilic vein; middle, graft interposed between superficial femoral artery and saphenous vein; bottom, various arrangements for AV grafts (straight, curved, loop). *Source:* From *Core Curriculum for Nephrology Nursing* (p. 234) by L.E. Lancaster, 1987, Pitman, NJ: American Nephrology Nurses' Association. Copyright 1987 by American Nephrology Nurses' Association. Reprinted by permission.

postoperative infection of the graft usually extends the entire length of the graft through the open space around the graft and frequently involves the suture lines; infection may lead to sacrifice of the graft, as it is very difficult to eradicate.

Thrombosis. Thrombosis causes venous outflow stenosis, inadequate arterial flow, extrinsic compression, and hemodynamic changes due to hypertension or hypovolemia. Venous outflow stenosis is surgically corrected by angioplasty or bypass grafts. Excessive pressure after needle removal and excessive ultrafiltration should be avoided. An adequate blood volume should be maintained.

Pseudoaneurysms and Aneurysms. Pseudoaneurysms can be prevented by achieving good hemostasis on needle removal, thus avoiding hematoma formation. Rotating puncture sites helps to prevent weakening of any one area of the graft and subsequent formation of aneurysms and pseudoaneurysms, both of which usually require surgical repair.

General Care and Patient Education

General care and patient education are the same as for internal AV fistulas except for vein maturation and techniques of care. Added emphasis should be placed on observing for infection and seeking prompt treatment. Techniques for achieving hemostasis without occlusive pressure should be practiced.

Temporary Devices

A device may be used on a temporary basis for vascular cannulation and circulatory access for hemodialysis until a permanent method can be prepared or until a different type of dialysis therapy can be instituted.

Indications for Temporary Devices

Temporary devices are indicated (1) when immediate access to the circulation is needed in patients with acute renal failure; (2) while waiting for an AV fistula or graft to mature; (3) after removal of a permanent access device because of infection; and (4) before initiation of peritoneal dialysis or during episodes of peritonitis. Temporary devices may be used for weeks or even months.

Types of Temporary Devices

Temporary devices are subclavian (e.g., Quinton, Vas-Cath). The subclavian vein is cannulated with a rigid or semirigid single-lumen or double-lumen catheter. The single-lumen catheter can be used for both the arterial source and the venous return by alternating flow controlled by a single-needle pump, or venous return may be via a peripheral vein or another site. The double-lumen catheter is used for both the arterial source and the venous return.

Insertion technique is the same as that for a central venous catheter placement. A chest x-ray is taken to confirm the position of the catheter.

Immediate postinsertion complications include traumatic pneumothorax, hemothorax, hydrothorax, inadvertent subclavian artery puncture, brachial plexus injury, and a sheared catheter with embolization. Other complications include air embolism, infection and sepsis, and clotting.

General Care and Patient Education

General care and patient education should include the following:

1. Use strict sterile technique when instituting and discontinuing hemodialysis.
2. Obtain blood cultures or catheter or skin exit site cultures (or all three) if any evidence of infection appears.
3. Heparinize the cannula after dialysis to ensure patency.
4. Change dressing over the catheter site daily; use sterile dressing and use antibiotic ointment around the exit site.
5. Use the catheter for hemodialysis only.
6. Secure placement of catheter caps after dialysis.

Femoral Vein Cannulation

Perform percutaneous cannulation of the femoral vein with one or more catheters; one catheter can be placed in each femoral vein for blood outflow and return; one catheter can be placed in a femoral vein with a peripheral vein used for return; or two catheters can be placed in one femoral vein.

COMPLICATIONS OF DIALYSIS

Dialysis Disequilibrium Syndrome

In dialysis disequilibrium syndrome, as a result of hemodialysis the concentration of the plasma urea nitrogen (BUN) is reduced more rapidly than the urea nitrogen in the cerebrospinal fluid and brain tissue. Because of the slow transport of urea across the blood-brain barrier, urea acts as an osmotic agent and draws water from the plasma and extracellular fluid into the cerebral cells, causing cerebral edema. Other factors that may cause this syndrome are rapid changes in pH and electrolyte shifts.

Signs and Symptoms

Signs and symptoms of dialysis disequilibrium syndrome include

- headache
- nausea
- vomiting
- restlessness
- hypertension
- increased pulse pressure
- decreased sensorium
- convulsions
- coma
- death

Prevention/Treatment

Dialysis disequilibrium syndrome can be prevented by short, frequent dialyses with a less efficient dialyzer and a slow rate of blood flow. The nurse should be alert to early signs and symptoms, and should terminate the dialysis procedure as soon as they appear. The addition of an osmotic solute, such as glucose, mannitol, urea, or sodium chloride, to the dialysate will prevent a rapid fall in plasma osmolality.

Dialysis Encephalopathy

Dialysis encephalopathy is caused by an accumulation of aluminum from water used to prepare dialysate or from the administration of aluminum-containing phosphate-binding medications.

Signs and Symptoms

Signs and symptoms of dialysis encephalopathy are

- alterations in behavior
- speech disturbances, apraxia, dysarthia, aphasia

- myoclonus
- seizures
- gait difficulty
- electroencephalographic (EEG) changes
- osteodystrophy
- anemia

Treatment

Treatment involves the use of treated water for dialysate preparation, and serum aluminum chelation with deferoxamine mesylate (Desferal). Discontinue oral aluminum-based medications used for phosphate binders and substitute nonaluminum preparations. Renal transplantation should be considered.

Air Embolism

Air embolism is caused by the introduction of a large quantity of air into the venous circulation. Causes include a defective or disarmed air detector or retention of air in the dialyzer resulting from an ineffective priming procedure; loose connections or leaks in the extracorporeal circuit; blood pump set too fast during reinfusion; empty intravenous bags, blood bags, or infusion syringes; and use of air-vented intravenous bottles.

Signs and Symptoms

Signs and symptoms include

- evidence of air in blood lines or entering the patient
- patient chest pain, dyspnea, coughing, cyanosis
- patient visual problems ("seeing stars," diplopia, blindness)
- patient neurologic deficits (confusion, coma, hemiparesis)
- patient death

Prevention

Preventive measures include the following precautions: Prime the dialyzer thoroughly with venous (outlet) end up to remove all air. Bridge and tape all connections securely and increase blood pump speed slowly. An air detector must be used at all times, but it is not foolproof. Reinfuse slowly, and have double clamps in position at all times. Do not air rinse.

During dialysis administer saline as a bolus, rather than as a constant infusion; observe blood and total parenteral nutrition infusions carefully. Discard clamps with weak jaws, and use bags rather than glass air-vented bottles.

Treatment

Immediately

- stop the infusion of air
- position the patient on the left side with feet elevated (Trendelenburg position) for at least 30 minutes
- assess vital signs
- administer oxygen
- notify the physician
- assess possible causes

Hemolysis

Hemolysis is caused by rupture of red blood cells as a result of hypotonic dialysate temperature. Hemolysis usually involves two simultaneous errors, including any of the following: failure to supply the delivery system with dialysate concentrate; obstruction of dialysate concentrate line; incorrect setting of conductivity alarm limits; absence of conductivity alarm (on older systems); malfunction of conductivity monitors; or malfunction of proportioning pumps.

Signs and Symptoms

Signs and symptoms include

- chest pain and dyspnea
- hypotension
- clear (cherry red) blood in venous line
- burning in circulatory return site
- warmth in throat
- arrhythmias
- low serum sodium concentration
- decreased hematocrit
- increased serum potassium concentration

Prevention

Prevention methods include a manual check of dialysate conductivity immediately before dialysis is initiated. The concentrate tank, lines, and filter should be cleaned frequently. Select a delivery system with a conductivity monitor and alarm with preset limits, and provide regular preventive maintenance of alarm systems.

Treatment

Treatment includes the following:

- clamp return (venous) line immediately; do not reinfuse hemolyzed blood
- monitor vital signs and observe for arrhythmias, hypotension, and dyspnea
- check hematocrit and electrolytes (Acute anemia is most often the critical problem; hyperkalemia develops secondary to hemolysis.)
- administer oxygen
- replace volume and consider blood transfusion if symptoms are severe
- administer hypertonic intravenous solutions if indicated
- repeat dialysis if electrolyte abnormalities are severe

Exsanguination

Exsanguination can be caused by accidental separation of blood lines; accidental dislodgment of needles from the circulatory access site; ruptured blood lines; ruptured dialyzer membrane; separation of the external cannula from the dialyzer or from the vessel; or internal bleeding.

Signs and Symptoms

Signs and symptoms include

- obvious source of bleeding
- shock, often with convulsions or vomiting, or both
- melena or hematemesis in gastrointestinal bleeding

Prevention

Preventive measures include the following precautions: Tightly secure and bridge all connections; tape needles at two points; do not allow the patient to dialyze alone; check the blood pump monthly for proper occlusion; and place blood lines in the pump properly.

All delivery systems should have a functioning blood leak detector, but dialysate outflow should be monitored visually for evidence of blood. Provide proper access care and observation, and use regional or tight heparinization if patient has a bleeding tendency.

Hyperthermia

Signs and Symptoms

Signs and symptoms of hyperthermia include

- patient complaints of feeling hot
- very dark blood
- eventual coma and death

Prevention

Prevention of hyperthermia includes ensuring that all electrical components are shielded from the corrosive effects of dialysate. Two temperature monitors should be present, one to control the heater and one to monitor the final temperature, and they should have regular preventive maintenance. Check dialysate temperature when the patient complains of feeling hot.

Treatment

Treatment is carried out as follows:

- discontinue dialysis immediately
- do not return heat-damaged blood
- obtain serial measurement of patient's temperature
- record temperature of the dialysate
- determine hematocrit and electrolyte levels
- observe for signs and symptoms of hemolysis
- provide external cooling for temperature over 106° F

Cardiac Tamponade

Causes of cardiac tamponade include acute pericarditis, chronic pericarditis, and constrictive pericarditis. Cardiac tamponade also may be precipitated by a reduction in blood volume or by heparin administration in the presence of any of the above conditions.

Signs and Symptoms

Signs and symptoms of cardiac tamponade are

- central chest pain, often worse when supine, improves when upright
- pericardial friction rub
- hypotension, especially during dialysis, often apparently inappropriate
- paradoxical pulse greater than 10 mm Hg
- distended neck veins
- muffled heart sounds
- absent apical impulse
- low electrocardiographic (ECG) voltage
- pulsus alternans
- decreasing level of consciousness

Prevention

Prevention requires the following measures: Auscultate for a friction rub and for a paradoxical pulse when the patient has chest pain or unexpectedly low blood pressure; dialyze using regional or tight heparinization when pericarditis is known; and maintain intravascular volume to avoid hypotension in a patient with known pericarditis.

Treatment

Treatment involves the following:

- intensive dialysis (often daily) for pericarditis
- subtotal pericardiectomy for pericardial effusion
- pericardiocentesis (in an extreme emergency while preparing the patient for surgery; a pericardiocentesis tray should be available at all times)

Cardiac Arrest

Causes of cardiac arrest include electrolyte imbalances, arrhythmias, myocardial infarction, cardiac tamponade, presence of a large air embolism, hemolysis, exsanguination, and hyperthermia.

Prevention

Prevent any conditions that could lead to cardiac arrest, and assess closely during dialysis. Provide ECG monitoring for patients at risk.

Fever

Fever is caused by pyrogens and infection.

Prevention

Prevention is obtained by proper water treatment, using proper technique for preparing and initiation of dialysis, and by protecting the patient from known infectious agents.

Treatment

Treatment involves the following actions:

- assess the patient for sources and signs of infection
- obtain blood cultures as ordered
- culture dialysate and product water
- administer aspirin or acetaminophen as ordered
- administer antibiotics as ordered

Seizures

Seizures may be caused by dialysis disequilibrium syndrome, electrolyte imbalances, hypotension, and dialysate composition errors.

Prevention

Seizures can be prevented by avoiding an excessively rapid BUN drop during dialysis and avoiding severe uremia; by administering anticonvulsant medication; and by providing blood pressure monitoring and support during dialysis.

Treatment

Treatment for seizures involves the following actions:

- slow the blood flow and shorten dialysis to decrease BUN slowly
- begin dialysis early in course of uremia

- measure blood pressure frequently during dialysis and administer volume expander as necessary

Arrhythmias

Arrhythmias are caused by electrolyte and pH changes, underlying heart disease, and removal of antiarrhythmic drugs by dialysis.

Prevention

Arrhythmias can be prevented by the use of 3-mEq potassium dialysate if the patient has known heart disease or is on a digitalis preparation. Additional antiarrhythmic drugs should be given during dialysis.

Treatment

Treatment involves the following actions:

- administer antiarrhythmic drugs as required
- administer potassium as required
- discontinue dialysis for severe, symptomatic arrhythmias
- monitor the ECG
- notify the physician

Headache, Cramps, Back Pain

Headaches, cramps, and back pain are caused by early disequilibrium syndrome or rapid ultrafiltration.

Prevention

Prevention is achieved by proper dietary control of urea nitrogen, fluid, and electrolytes and by avoidance of rapid dialysis.

Treatment

Headache, cramps, and back pain can be alleviated by

- slowing the blood flow
- administering saline intravenously
- ultrafiltering without diffusing during the first hour of dialysis

Angina

The main cause of angina is anemia.

Prevention

Angina can be avoided by blood transfusion if necessary, administration of nitroglycerin or related drugs, and increasing blood pump speed slowly.

Treatment

Angina is treated as follows:

- discontinue dialysis if severe
- administer oxygen
- administer nitroglycerin
- administer a mild sedative
- decrease blood flow
- decrease ultrafiltration rate

Hypotension

Causes of hypotension include use of antihypertensive medications, inadequate sodium in the diet, unstable cardiovascular status, hypoalbuminemia, and hypovolemia resulting from excessive fluid and sodium removal during dialysis.

Prevention

Hypotension can be prevented by proper fluid and sodium intake between dialyses, withholding antihypertensive medications immediately before and during dialysis, maintaining an adequate hematocrit, treating cardiovascular problems, performing ultrafiltration as slowly as possible, using bicarbonate rather than acetate as a buffer in the dialysate, performing ultrafiltration without diffusion, and teaching the patient to recognize early signs and symptoms.

Treatment

Hypotension can be treated by decreasing the rate of blood flow from the patient to the dialyzer and lowering the transmembrane pressure to decrease ultrafiltration and thus the amount of fluid removed from the intravascular volume. The patient's feet and legs should be elevated above the level of the heart; this returns approximately 500 mL/minute to the heart.

Increase the circulating fluid volume by administering normal saline boluses (100 to 500 mL) into the blood lines; frequent blood pressure measurements must be made during this administration.

Increase the circulating fluid volume by administering a colloid osmotic agent, such as albumin or mannitol, to create an osmotic gradient. Albumin and mannitol cause fluid to move from the extravascular space into the vascular space. Albumin is especially helpful in increasing the blood pressure in a patient with a low serum albumin. If the patient has significant edema, albumin or mannitol pulls the edema fluid into the vascular space for removal by ultrafiltration. In this situation, albumin or mannitol should be given early during dialysis so that the excess fluid is removed before completion of dialysis. Otherwise, the excess vascular fluid volume can lead to pulmonary edema.

Increase the circulating fluid volume by administering hypertonic sodium chloride, which causes fluid to move from the extravascular space into the vascular space, to increase the vascular volume and increase the blood pressure.

Consider blood transfusion for a patient with a low hematocrit.

Hepatitis

The patient on hemodialysis has an increased risk of developing hepatitis. Different types of hepatitis are described in Table 5-1.

Table 5-1 Types of Hepatitis

Type	Mode of Transmission	Diagnostic Criteria	Comments
Hepatitis A	Fecal-oral route	Appearance of IgM, hepatitis A virus in the serum	Generally not a problem in dialysis patients
Hepatitis B	Blood transfusions; needle sticks	HBsAg (surface antigen); HBcAg (core antigen)	
Non-A, non-B	Parenteral exposure	No specific diagnostic tests available	Most common form of hepatitis found in dialysis facilities

UREA KINETIC MODELING

The patient on hemodialysis may now have available a more precise and tailored dialysis because of the concept of urea kinetic modeling. The urea kinetic model is a mathematic description of the generation and removal of urea in prerenal dialysis patients. By considering the patient-specific parameters that affect BUN, dialysis treatment can be quantified and tailored to individual needs.

CONTINUOUS AV HEMOFILTRATION

Continuous AV hemofiltration (CAVH) uses the patient's arterial blood pressure and not an external pump to deliver blood to a low-resistance hemodialyzer, primarily for water removal. Hemofiltration is an effective method of ultrafiltration in both acute and chronic renal failure. It may also be used in conjunction with hemodialysis and as a method of volume loss to allow the patient to be hemodialyzed less frequently for solute removal. This approach is better tolerated by the critically ill patient who is unable to cope with the aggressive ultrafiltration and other side effects associated with hemodialysis (Kaplan et al., 1984; Williams & Perkins, 1984).

Principles of Action

Hemofiltration is based on the principles of filtration and convection.

Filtration

Filtration is the movement of fluid across a semipermeable membrane from an area of greater pressure to one of lesser pressure.

Convection

In convection, elements in the plasma water are conveyed across the semipermeable filter as a result of differences in hydrostatic pressure in the hemofiltration system. The ultrafiltrate that is removed is a fluid that is free of protein and red blood cells and contains potassium, sodium, chloride, glucose, urea, and creatinine in amounts equal to the concentrations present in the patient's plasma. Lower levels of calcium are found in the filtrate, because a percentage of this ion is bound to protein.

The relative clearance of nutrients such as amino acids and glucose is less of a problem because any element larger than 10,000 d is retained by the filter in CAVH. Albumin, other proteins, and protein-bound substances are retained in the plasma and returned to the patient.

Intermediate molecules such as glucose and some vitamins are conveyed according to time limits. The longer it takes for the patient's own blood to clear the filter, the more likely that intermediate molecules will be filtered out of the patient's system. (See Figure 5-8.)

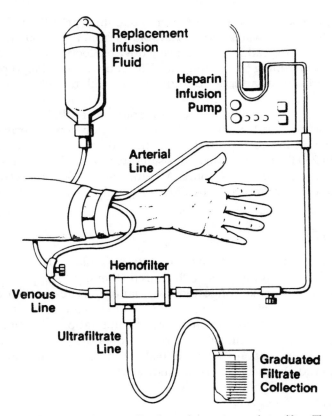

Figure 5-8 CAVH system using a small-volume, low-resistance hemofilter. The arterial tubing is color-coded red, and the venous tubing blue. Blood flows from the arterial shunt into the arterial hemofilter tubing, where it is heparinized. A second infusion port in the arterial tubing is used for flushing the hemofilter when clotting occurs. Blood specimens may be obtained from ports on both the arterial and venous sides of the hemofilter. Replacement intravenous solution is infused into the venous infusion port. A sterile, metered, urinary drainage bag is connected to the ultrafiltration line, to collect fluid removed from the patient. *Source:* From "Preventing Complications in Continuous Arteriovenous Hemofiltration" by A.A. Whittaker et al., 1986, *Dimensions of Critical Care Nursing, 15,* p. 74. Copyright 1986 by J.B. Lippincott Company. Reprinted by permission.

Small molecules such as creatinine are not conveyed across the filter.

Based on the principle of convection, hemofiltration removes filterable solutes in proportion to plasma water. Large amounts of plasma water removed result in large amounts of filterable solutes removed.

CAVH Process

In CAVH, blood flows from an arterial site through a filter. The filter separates the plasma water and certain solutes from the blood and passes the ultrafiltrate to a graduated measuring device. Blood free of ultrafiltrate returns through tubing to a venous site. The patient's own blood pressure forces blood from the arterial insertion site through the tubing to the venous site.

Ultrafiltrate is producible with an AV gradient resulting from a mean arterial pressure (MAP) of 60 mm Hg. A higher blood pressure and blood flow rate result in greater ultrafiltrate. (Hemodialysis requires a blood flow rate of 250 to 300 mL/min and is safest with a MAP of 75 mm Hg.)

CAVH can filter 20 L in 24 hours. A pump can be used to speed up the filtration rate. The pump is applied to the arterial transport tubing (Figure 5-9).

Indications for CAVH

CAVH is indicated for patients with hypervolemia with or without renal failure who are unresponsive to diuretic therapy (e.g., patients with acute pulmonary edema, congestive heart failure, ascites, and chronic renal failure); for patients with oliguria who require large quantities of parenteral fluids (e.g., hyperalimentation, administration of antibiotics in fluid, or continuous administration of vasopressors); and for hemodynamically unstable patients who are unable to tolerate hemodialysis and in whom peritoneal dialysis is contraindicated.

Contraindications for CAVH

CAVH should not be used in patients who have a hematocrit greater than 45% or who cannot tolerate anticoagulation, since either of these conditions can precipitate clotting of the hemofilter (Keily, 1984).

Vascular Access

A number of AV access devices can be used for CAVH, such as a femoral or subclavian catheter. Other types of vascular access devices also can be used, including an AV shunt or an AV fistula. The diameter and poten-

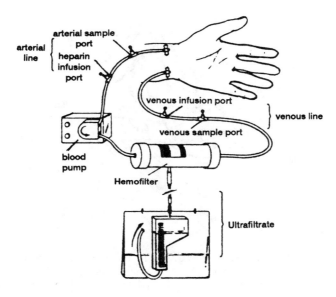

Figure 5-9 Use of a blood pump with CAVH. *Source:* From "Hemofiltration: A New Technique in Critical Care Nursing" by C. Winkelman, 1985, *Heart and Lung, 14,* p. 267. Copyright 1985 by The C.V. Mosby Company. Reprinted by permission.

tial flow rate of an access device are important considerations in selecting an access source because both factors can affect the success of the procedure. Other factors that affect ultrafiltration are the osmolality of the blood, arterial blood pressure, the degree of negative pressure, and the hydration status of the blood. Usually, femoral vessels are used with an arterial catheter placed in one lower extremity and a venous catheter placed in the other lower extremity (Figure 5-10).

Heparinization

The arteriovenous tubing and filter should be primed with a heparin-saline solution (2 L of saline and 5000 U of heparin) (Paganini & Nakamoto, 1983). This procedure eliminates air bubbles; the saline also rinses the filter (Henderson et al., 1983).

An initial bolus of 1000 to 3000 U of heparin is then given via the arterial port. Heparin is continuously infused via a perfusion pump through the same port at a usual dose of 500 to 1000 U/hour. Such heparinization is

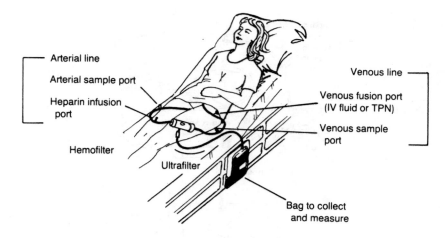

Figure 5-10 Method and devices used for CAVH. IV, Intravenous; TPN, total parenteral nutrition. *Source:* From "Hemofiltration: A New Technique in Critical Care Nursing" by C. Winkelman, 1985, *Heart and Lung, 14,* p. 266. Copyright 1985 by The C.V. Mosby Company. Reprinted by permission.

necessary to prevent clotting with extracorporeal tubing and the hemofilter.

Activated clotting times (ACT) or whole-blood partial thromboplastin time can be used to monitor the patient's clotting time, and the heparin infusion is adjusted accordingly (Figure 5-11). ACT is a method of evaluating whole-blood clotting. The exact procedure for obtaining an ACT varies according to the brand of ACT monitoring device being used. The normal ACT is 90 to 150 seconds. To prevent hemofilter clotting during CAVH, the ACT should be kept between 100 and 300 seconds.

CAVH Set-Up

Ports

A port at the venous end of the transport tubing is used to withdraw blood samples (postfilter). Another venous port can be used as an access through which to infuse fluids, including some hypertonic solutions. A third port is connected to a graduated container and is used to collect and measure the ultrafiltrate. A screw clamp can be used on the tubing that

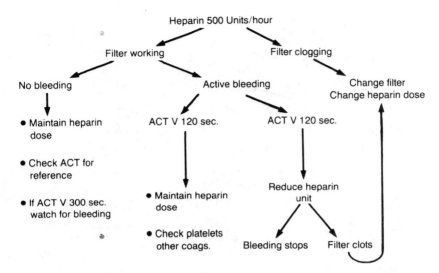

Figure 5-11 Heparin flow chart. *Source:* From "Nursing Management of Continuous Arteriovenous Hemofiltration for Acute Renal Failure" by J.C. Palmer et al., 1986, *Focus on Critical Care, 13*, p. 27. Copyright 1986 by The C.V. Mosby Company. Reprinted by permission.

connects the filter to the measuring device to permit adjustment of the amount of ultrafiltrate being removed. Closure of the clamp allows less ultrafiltrate to be removed; opening the clamp allows greater amounts of ultrafiltrate to be collected and discarded.

Adjusting the position of the measuring container in relation to the filter changes the amount of ultrafiltrate produced. Lowering the container below the filter creates a negative pressure on the system (Figure 5-12).

Nursing Care during CAVH

During CAVH the nurse should

- assist with set-up and priming of the system
- maintain blood flow and asepsis in the system
- monitor clotting times (partial thromboplastin times) through use of ACTs
- adjust heparin infusion rate as necessary
- assess heparin dosage and intravenous rate every hour and as required

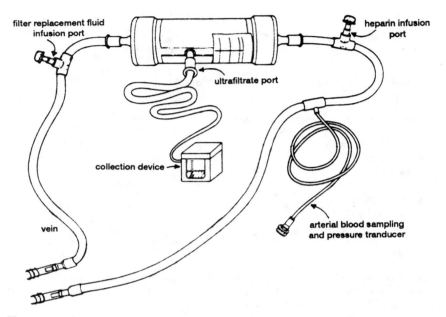

Figure 5-12 CAVH circuit. *Source:* From "Nursing Management of Continuous Arterio-venous Hemofiltration for Acute Renal Failure" by J.C. Palmer et al., 1986, *Focus on Critical Care, 13,* p. 23. Copyright 1986 by The C.V. Mosby Company. Reprinted by permission.

- report bleeding from access sites to the physician
- avoid unnecessary bleeding by not inserting or removing intravenous or arterial lines while heparin is infusing
- manage fluid replacement as prescribed by the physician
- monitor laboratory values
    1. assess electrolytes every 4 to 6 hours (Special attention should be given to electrolytes whose imbalance may cause cardiac dysrhythmias, tetany, or acidosis [i.e., hyperkalemia, hypocalcemia].)
- monitor intake and output (Patients may receive more intravenous fluids or drink more fluids since a fluid restriction is not required.)
    1. monitor amount and color of ultrafiltrate and record every hour (Ultrafiltrate may be measured with a urinary drainage bag or with an electronic meter.)
- record patient's weight daily
- monitor vital signs

1. assess blood pressure every 30 to 60 minutes (A decreased blood pressure leads to a slower blood flow and may cause the hemo-filter to clot.)
2. assess for shock secondary to decreased intravascular volume
- perform shunt or catheter care
  1. inspect insertion sites every shift for signs of inflammation
  2. inspect insertion sites every day and as required, according to hospital policy
  3. perform dressing changes every day and as required, according to hospital policy
- assess for signs/symptoms of infection (i.e., fever, redness at the in-sertion sites, increased white blood cells)
- change the system every 24 hours (The system should also be changed if the casing cracks or if the membrane providing resistance to blood flow is ruptured.)
  1. inspect the access site
  2. palpate the access for a thrill or auscultate for a bruit (Access should also be warm to the touch.)
- educate the patient/family

Changing the Hemofiltration System

The tubing and hemofilter need to be replaced when the hemofiltration system is no longer patent or the ultrafiltrate production decreases to 50% or less of baseline.

Priming the new set-up involves the following steps:

1. stop the heparin infusion
2. clamp the ultrafiltrate port
3. clamp arterial and venous lines
4. swab connections with povidone-iodine
5. disconnect arterial line from tubing (with sterile gloves) and flush with 10 mL of saline; attach arterial end to a 500-mL bag of normal saline
6. clamp arterial and venous lines and return blood to patient by gravity (Recovery of red blood cells is enhanced if the filter is held vertically with the venous side lower than the arterial side.)
   — clamp and release the arterial side to assist in blood return; never clamp and release the venous side

— observe for clots or air

— clamp the venous line and disconnect transport tubing

Venous and arterial cannulas may or may not be disconnected depending on the patient's needs and physician orders.

Advantages of CAVH over hemodialysis are that it allows the elimination of large amounts of fluid without the osmolar changes associated with hemodialysis; it preserves extracellular fluid status (Golper, 1985); it preserves cardiovascular stability; and it does not reduce the patient's platelet and white blood cell count because it avoids the use of a membrane that might cause these problems (e.g., Cuprophane, cellulose acetate, or regenerated cellulose).

The disadvantage of CAVH over hemodialysis is that CAVH has a limited ability to remove wastes and excess solute with minimal volume replacement.

REFERENCES

Golper, T.A. (1985). Continuous arteriovenous hemofiltration in acute renal failure. *American Journal of Kidney Disease, 6*(6), 373–386.

Henderson, A.E., Donald, L.L., & Levin, N.W. (1983). Clinical use of the Amicon Diafilter. *Dialysis & Transplantation, 12*, 523–525.

Kaplan, A., Longnecker, R.E., & Folkert, V.W. (1984). Continuous arteriovenous hemofiltration: A report of six months experience. *Annals of Internal Medicine, 100*(3), 358–367.

Keily, M. (1984). Continuous arteriovenous hemofiltration. *Critical Care Nurse, 4*, 39–43.

Paganini, E.P., & Nakamoto, S. (1983). Continuous slow ultrafiltration in oliguric acute renal failure. *Transactions of the American Society for Artificial Internal Organs, 26*, 201.

Williams, V., & Perkins, L. (1984). Continuous ultrafiltration, a new ICU procedure for the treatment of fluid overload. *Critical Care Nurse, 4*, 44–49.

SUGGESTED READINGS

Lancaster, L.E. (1984). *The patient with end stage renal disease* (2nd ed.). New York: Wiley.

Lancaster, L.E., Binkley, L.S., & Keen, M. (1987). Concepts and principles of hemodialysis. In L.E. Lancaster (Ed.), *Core curriculum for nephrology nursing*. Pitman, NJ: American Nephrology Nurses' Association.

Stark, J.L. (1988). Chronic renal failure. In M.R. Kinney, D.R. Packa, & S.B. Dunbar (Eds.), *AACN's clinical reference for critical care nursing* (2nd ed.). New York: McGraw-Hill.

6

Peritoneal Dialysis

ANATOMY AND PHYSIOLOGY

The peritoneum is a serous membrane that covers the abdominal organs and lines the abdominal wall. The peritoneal membrane is 1 to 2 m². The peritoneal membrane consists of the vascular wall, interstitium, mesothelium, and adjacent fluid films. The parietal peritoneum receives its blood supply from the arteries of the abdominal wall. The blood from the parietal peritoneum and abdominal wall drains into the systemic circulation. The visceral peritoneum receives its blood supply from the mesenteric and celiac arteries. Blood from the visceral peritoneum converges and enters the portal vein (Figure 6-1).

Peritoneal dialysis involves the principles of osmosis and diffusion. Diffusion involves the movement of solutes across the peritoneal membrane from an area of higher solute concentration to an area of lower solute concentration.

Factors that influence solute transport are

- peritoneal permeability
  1. inflammation, especially peritonitis
  2. drugs
  3. collagen disease or vascular disease (or both) and membrane abnormalities
- solute characteristics
  1. size
  2. electrical charge
  3. water versus lipid solubility
  4. protein binding

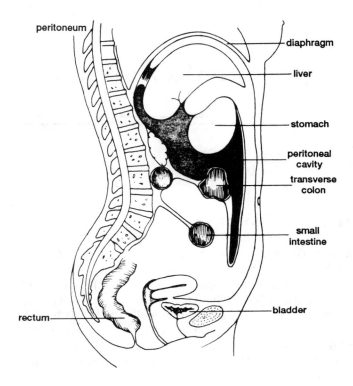

Figure 6-1 Location of the peritoneum in relation to other internal organs. *Source:* From *Renal Problems in Critical Care* (p. 132) by L. Schoengrund and P. Balzer (Eds.), 1985, New York: John Wiley and Sons, Inc. Copyright 1985 by Delmar Publishers, Inc. Reprinted by permission.

5. concentration gradient
6. peritoneal blood flow
7. temperature of dialysis solution
8. available membrane area (decreased by scarring or adhesions)

Factors that enhance diffusion are

- increased dialysis solution flow
- increased blood flow
- high concentration gradient
- prewarmed dialysis solution

- osmotic pressure (creates a solvent drag that pulls additional solute across the membrane)

Substances lost in the dialysate include

- proteins
- amino acids
- water-soluble vitamins
- trace minerals
- some hormones (e.g., parathyroid hormone)
- some drugs

Substances absorbed from the dialysate into the systemic circulation include

- dextrose
- calcium

Osmosis through the peritoneal membrane is the movement of water across the peritoneal membrane from an area of lower solute concentration to an area of higher solute concentration. Factors that influence water removal are

- surface area
- peritoneal membrane permeability
- colloid osmotic and oncotic pressure
- hydrostatic pressure gradient
- osmotic pressure gradient (dextrose concentration)
- dwell time

Ultrafiltration is defined as water removed as related to an osmotic pressure gradient.

Dextrose is added to the dialysis solution to create an osmotic gradient. The ultrafiltration rate is highest at the beginning of each exchange, when the osmotic gradient is highest. Ultrafiltration volume peaks when the dialysate osmolarity has decreased to equal the serum osmolality (due to dextrose absorption). Water is reabsorbed if the dialysate is allowed to dwell past the osmotic equilibrium.

Dextrose solutions containing 1.5% dextrose will approximately equal the combined colloid and hydrostatic pressure on the blood side, resulting in little or no fluid removal. Dextrose solutions of 2.5% and 4.25% are hypertonic and are used to increase ultrafiltration. Persistent use of hypertonic dialysis solution may increase the serum osmolality or cause hypovolemia (or both), leading to excessive thirst that leads to increased fluid intake, necessitating more ultrafiltration. Dialysis solutions that contain more than 4.25 g of dextrose per deciliter cause fast water removal, which causes an increased serum osmolality that results in hypernatremia, hypovolemic shock, or dialysis disequilibrium. Different exchange volumes and dextrose concentrations cause patterns of ultrafiltration.

PATIENT SELECTION FOR PERITONEAL DIALYSIS

Peritoneal dialysis is preferred in

- small children in whom vascular access is difficult and hemodialysis would be traumatic
- patients with severe cardiac disease
- patients for whom hemodialysis is contraindicated

Absolute contraindications to peritoneal dialysis include

- hypercatabolism (peritoneal dialysis is unable to remove uremic metabolites adequately)
- patent opening between peritoneal and pleural cavities
- inadequate transfer surface area due to scarring and adhesions (i.e., from multiple surgeries, previous peritonitis)

Relative contraindications to chronic peritoneal dialysis include

- morbid obesity
- chronic low back pain
- history of ruptured diverticuli
- infected abdominal vascular graft
- abdominal disease or malignancy
- significant respiratory insufficiency
- unrepaired hernia

PERITONEAL DIALYSIS PROCESS

Peritoneal dialysis is accomplished through the exchange or cycling of dialysis fluid through the peritoneal cavity. An exchange or cycle is composed of the infusion, dwell, and drainage of a specific volume of dialysis solution; exchanges or cycles are repeated throughout the course of dialysis.

The infusion step of the exchange is completed by allowing a specified volume of dialysis solution to flow into the peritoneal cavity by gravity with a manual or cycling system. Infusion or inflow of fluid by gravity takes approximately 10 minutes (for a 2-L volume).

Factors that affect the rate of inflow by gravity include the height of the solution, the inner diameter of the tubing, the tubing length, and intra-abdominal pressure.

The dwell step of the exchange is the period of time provided for diffusion and osmosis to take place. For manual dialysis, a typical dwell time is 10 to 30 minutes; in continuous dialysis, the dwell time is several hours.

Drainage of the fluid from the peritoneal cavity by gravity completes the exchange process. Drainage of 2 L (plus ultrafiltrate) takes about 10 minutes if the catheter is functioning optimally.

Factors that affect the drain rate include the position of the catheter, internal or external occlusion of the lines, intra-abdominal pressure, the tubing diameter, tubing length, and height distance from the abdomen to the drain bag.

ACUTE PERITONEAL DIALYSIS

Acute peritoneal dialysis can be instituted at the patient's bedside. Patients who are hemodynamically unstable or who have overdosed on drugs that are primarily protein bound may require acute peritoneal dialysis.

Acute Catheters

Rigid Stylet

The rigid stylet is intended for acute use only. This catheter can be inserted by the physician at the bedside so that dialysis can be initiated immediately. Because the catheter is rigid, there is an increased risk of organ perforation, and the insertion may be uncomfortable for the patient. Other disadvantages of this approach include an increased incidence of dialysate leak, a risk of intraperitoneal catheter loss, an increased risk of infection with length of dialysis, and the need for repeated insertion of the catheter for each acute dialysis.

Single-Cuff Silicone Rubber Catheter

The single-cuff silicone rubber catheter can be inserted at the bedside by the physician, using a trocar or peritoneoscope, or it can be placed surgically under direct vision. The advantages of using this type of catheter include a decreased risk of organ perforation, increased comfort for the patient, and long-term usability if necessary for chronic dialysis (Figure 6-2).

Catheter Insertion

Preoperative nursing care should

- educate the patient
- ensure that the patient's bladder is empty (decreases the risk of perforation)

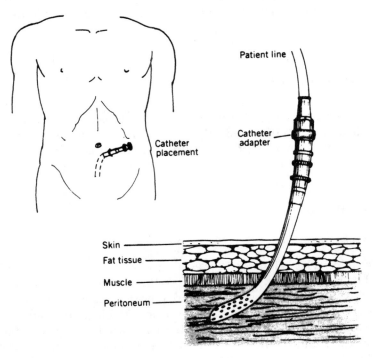

Figure 6-2 Placement of catheter into the peritoneal cavity. *Source:* From *Renal Problems in Critical Care* (p. 138) by L. Schoengrund and P. Balzer (Eds.), 1985, New York: John Wiley and Sons, Inc. Copyright 1985 by Delmar Publishers, Inc. Reprinted by permission.

- relieve patient's constipation (decreases the risk of bowel perforation)
- administer prophylactic antibiotics as ordered (usually given intravenously preoperatively), e.g.,
    1. vancomycin hydrochloride, single dose
    2. cephalosporin, single dose (may be followed by a short course of oral therapy)
    3. cephalosporin and aminoglycoside
- record baseline weight and vital signs

Insertion procedure for acute stylet catheter insertion provides that

- staff must mask, scrub, gown, and glove
- patient's abdomen is scrubbed with povidone-iodine solution and draped
- skin and subcutaneous tissues are infiltrated with a local anesthetic
- a small stab wound is made 3 to 5 cm below the umbilicus
- a stylet or large-bore blunt needle is inserted through the incision

The patient is asked to raise his or her head and neck to tighten the abdominal muscles to increase the intra-abdominal pressure; the peritoneal membrane is then punctured. An audible pop can be heard and there is noticeably less resistance. Dialysis solution is infused; this provides a cushion of fluid anterior to the mesentery and bowel, which decreases the risk of trauma during the positioning of the peritoneal catheter. At this point

- the catheter is maneuvered into place
- the skin is closed with purse-string sutures
- antibacterial ointment is applied to the incision site
- sterile dressings are applied

Peritoneoscopic insertion procedure (may be used for insertion of Tenckhoff-type catheters for acute or chronic use) provides that

- staff must mask, scrub, gown, and glove
- premedication is given as ordered by the physician
- patient's abdomen is prepared and draped
- skin and subcutaneous tissue are infiltrated with local anesthetic

An incision is made into the skin and a blunt dissection is made with a hemostat to the abdominal wall. The sterile peritoneoscope is assembled and blindly inserted into the peritoneal cavity with the trocar (less than 3 mm diameter). The trocar is removed, the needlescope is inserted, and the operator inspects local peritoneal surfaces to document intraperitoneal location. The needlescope is withdrawn and 1 L of air is insufflated. The needlescope with cannula and catheter guide is reinserted and advanced as far as possible into the pelvis (adhesions can be visualized and avoided). If the scope cannot be fully inserted, the patient is placed in the Trendelenburg position.

If the scope still cannot be inserted fully, the catheter is shortened correspondingly. The needlescope and cannula are removed, leaving the catheter guide. The catheter guide is dilated with 4- and 6-mm rods and the catheter is inserted; the guide and obturator are removed. A subcutaneous tunnel is formed, using a uterine sound or the catheter guide. The skin exit site is located, anesthetized, and formed by a stab incision. The cannula and trocar are advanced through the exit incision, leaving the catheter guide in place. The tract for the subcutaneous cuff is dilated and the catheter is pulled through the exit site until the cuff reaches the appropriate position. Dialysis solution is infused to assess for patency and leaks. Subcutaneous tissue and skin are sutured, and sterile dressings are applied.

Initiation of Dialysis

Stylet Catheter

Dialysis is initiated after the connection of the tubing to the catheter. The exit site is protected with disinfecting ointment and sterile dressings.

Silastic Catheter

Intermittent peritoneal dialysis with full volume exchanges can be initiated within a few days to a week after catheter implementation. Continuous dialysis should be delayed for 10 to 14 days to allow wound healing and tissue ingrowth.

Manual Dialysis Exchanges

The nurse must warm the dialysis solution, spike and hang each exchange, and control the cycle phases manually. Measured temperature should be approximately 37° C. Water baths are not recommended for heating peritoneal dialysis solution because of the increased risk of contamination to the system. Dry heating is the preferred method. Dry heating methods include the use of a heating pad, heating cabinet, or microwave oven. Home dialysis patients may place the plastic bottle or bag in an overwrap on or near a home-heating source or in the sunshine.

Addition of Medications

Heparin and potassium chloride are almost always used in acute peritoneal dialysis. Aseptic technique is critical in adding medications to the bottles or bags. Medications should be added immediately before the solution will be hung and used. The dialysis solution should be mixed well after medication has been added.

Hanging Solution Containers

An aseptic procedure should be followed when spiking and hanging solution containers. The nurse and the patient should mask. Handwashing should be done by the person hanging the fluid. A povidone-iodine shield or wrap may be used to protect the external connection.

To infuse fluid, the solution container clamp and the patient line clamp are opened. The solution container clamp should be closed when the solution has completely infused to prevent infusion of air.

To initiate drain, the patient line clamp and the drain bag clamp are opened. Drainage is measured and discarded. Gloves should be worn when handling dialysate because it is considered a contaminated body fluid which may contain hepatitis and other viruses.

Nursing Assessment during Acute Peritoneal Dialysis

1. Record baseline vital signs and weight.
2. Observe the dialysate effluent immediately after catheter insertion. The effluent may be pink-tinged but should become clear to light yellow after the first few exchanges. Effluent may be frothy because of protein content. Effluent should be odorless.
3. Record fluid balance.
   — Record dialysis fluid balance for each exchange (volume in minus volume out).
   — Record cumulative dialysis fluid balance.
   — Record total fluid balance (all sources of intake and all routes of fluid loss).
4. Monitor vital signs and weight frequently; record supine and upright blood pressures.

5. Monitor blood chemistries, especially serum potassium, in order to determine when to add potassium to the dialysis solution and to assess the appropriateness of dosage.
6. Observe for complications of peritoneal dialysis.

Exit Site Care

Care of the exit site is important in preventing wound contamination, promoting healing by preventing wound contamination, promoting healing by preventing catheter movement, and preventing periluminal catheter contamination.

Sterile dressings should be performed until the exit site is healed and epithelialized. The nurse should cleanse the wound with hydrogen peroxide (cleansing with povidone-iodine is optional) and apply a sterile dressing. A mask should be worn when performing sterile dressing changes.

The exit site should be examined for

- bleeding
- scab formation
- crust formation
- fat necrosis (clear, sticky exudate)
- signs of an exit or tunnel infection
  1. erythema
  2. induration
  3. exudate
  4. unusual tenderness or pain
- cuff extrusion
- dialysate leak
  1. clear drainage
  2. blood glucose strip positive for glucose

Chronic Exit Site Care

Daily exit site care is recommended to prevent exit site infection. It can be done in conjunction with a shower or bath. The exit site should not be submerged in bathwater.

Exit site care components include

- cleansing options
  1. soap and water (an antibacterial soap is recommended)

   2. pHisoHex or povidone-iodine scrub
   3. povidone-iodine scrub plus hydrogen peroxide
- dressing options
   1. light gauze dressings
   2. air-occlusive dressings
   3. no dressings

The catheter or proximal connecting tubing should be secured to avoid tension and traction during procedures to prevent accidental trauma. A healthy exit site can be promoted by

- handwashing before touching the catheter
- good personal hygiene
- keeping skin folds clean and dry
- daily examination and evaluation of the exit site
- keeping the exit site dry
- preventing tape irritation
- stabilizing the catheter

Substances or conditions that are detrimental to the exit site include

- alcohol
- powders
- oil-based ointments
- dirty skin
- perspiration and moisture
- submersion in water
- extensive crust formation
- pressure from tight clothing
- scratching
- tension and pulling on the catheter

The exit site should be assessed daily by the patient or at each contact by the nursing staff. Inspection of the exit site should take note of the following:

- evidence of healing
   1. epithelialization
   2. granulation tissue

- color of a healed, healthy exit site
  1. same color as surrounding skin
  2. pink discoloration similar to healing scar
  3. brown discoloration
  4. dull, purplish discoloration
- crust formation from dried exudate (although ideally the exit site should not have crust formation)
- inflammation
  1. redness and irritation
  2. etiology
     —tight clothing
     —reaction to cleansing agents
     —developing infection
- infection
- cuff extrusion
- catheter condition
  1. wear lines and cracks
  2. adapter fully inserted and fits tightly

The adapter-tubing connection should be tight if the patient is using a wearable, continuous ambulatory peritoneal dialysis system.

Care of Inflamed or Infected Exit Site

Daily site care is recommended for inflamed or infected exit sites. A scab or crust should be removed gradually, not forcibly; hydrogen peroxide may be helpful, although it may need to be diluted to prevent irritation. Determine whether cleansing agents or povidone-iodine may be irritating the exit site, and keep the exit site dry. A light sterile dressing may protect against further contamination. Exuberant granulation tissue can be cauterized with silver nitrate. Topical disinfection or water-based antibiotic ointment may be used on the infected site.

OPTIONAL MODES OF PERITONEAL DIALYSIS

There are various modes of peritoneal dialysis. Three options currently available are intermittent peritoneal dialysis, continuous cyclic peritoneal dialysis, and continuous ambulatory peritoneal dialysis.

Intermittent Peritoneal Dialysis

Intermittent peritoneal dialysis (IPD) is a periodic dialysis with no solution dwelling in the peritoneal cavity between dialyses. Indications for IPD (Twandowski et al., 1986) include problems related to increased abdominal pressure, such as leaks, hernias, hemorrhoids, and poor appetite; rapid glucose absorption and poor ultrafiltration; and psychosocial indications, such as poor body image with chronic dialysis, and inability to perform daytime exchanges.

IPD can be done for 10 to 14 hours three or four times per week; for 8 to 12 hours nightly; or for 24 to 48 hours (for hospitalized patients).

Automated delivery systems are available to control the cycles automatically. Various cycler machines are available for patient use. The advantages of using cyclers are that the machine is relatively simple and inexpensive to operate, it can be operated independently by the patient, and some cyclers can be disassembled to become portable. The disadvantages of using cyclers are that prepared solutions and tubing are expensive, and the multiple connections to dialysis solution containers increase the risk of contamination.

Continuous Cyclic Peritoneal Dialysis

Continuous cyclic peritoneal dialysis (CCPD) uses a cycler for overnight exchanges and a long-dwell daytime exchange. CCPD usually involves three to four overnight cycles that have a dwell time of 2 to 3 hours. The daytime exchange lasts for 14 to 15 hours; use of hypertonic solution prevents significant reabsorption.

Continuous Ambulatory Peritoneal Dialysis

Continuous ambulatory peritoneal dialysis (CAPD) gives continuous dialysis with three to five daily exchanges. Dialysis solution is always present in the peritoneal cavity except for brief interruptions to drain and reinfuse or inflow. Dialysis is constant 24 hours a day, 7 days a week. Daytime exchanges last for 4 to 6 hours. Overnight exchanges last for 8 to 12 hours. A typical pattern is to exchange the solution on arising, at lunchtime, before or after dinner, and at bedtime. Several systems are available.

FACTORS THAT AFFECT INDIVIDUAL PERITONEAL DIALYSIS PRESCRIPTION

Patient factors that affect dialysis prescription include

- size
- metabolic rate
- residual renal function
- peritoneal membrane function
- physical or learning handicaps
- availability of a partner, assistant, or support personnel
- previous problems or complications

Other factors that affect dialysis prescription include

- systems and training program availability
- compatible solution volumes

PATIENT SELECTION FOR SELF-CARE PERITONEAL DIALYSIS

Chronic peritoneal dialysis is almost exclusively a home dialysis therapy. Assessment of self-care of a home dialysis candidate should include

- patient's understanding of the diagnosis of end-stage renal disease and therapy options
- patient's motivation for choosing home dialysis
- family support for patient's decision
- patient's past experiences with self-care
- level of independence in activities of daily living
- premorbid roles and level of functioning
- complexity of illness and degree of disability
- physical abilities or handicaps, including vision, muscle strength, and fine motor coordination
- family and community resources for assistance and support
- availability of a partner (if required) to perform some or all of the assessments or procedures; partner's willingness and motivation to assist the patient with dialysis

- patient's and/or partner's decision-making abilities
- physical details of the home
  1. access to electricity and/or water supply and drain for automated equipment
  2. space for supply storage
  3. size versus number of inhabitants (Is there an area that can be isolated for aseptic procedures?)

INFECTIOUS COMPLICATIONS OF PERITONEAL DIALYSIS

Peritonitis

Peritonitis is an inflammation of the peritoneum that can be divided into the categories of infectious peritonitis (caused by microorganisms), refractory or resistant peritonitis (symptoms do not abate after 48 hours of appropriate therapy), or relapsing or recurrent peritonitis (recurrence within 2 weeks of the completion of antibiotic therapy). In each case the organism and sensitivities must be identified.

There are several portals of entry for the causative organism.

Transluminal Entry. In transluminal entry, contamination is due to a break in the integrity of the closed system that occurs during an exchange or tube change and is most commonly caused by *Staphylococcus* species.

Periluminal Entry. In periluminal entry, contamination occurs along the outer surface of the catheter. The risk of periluminal contamination is increased with acute catheter use, leak, or frank bleed. The organisms most commonly identified are *Staphylococcus* species and *Pseudomonas* species.

Hematogenous Entry. Hematogenous infection is caused by transient bacteremia. It is sometimes associated with dental procedures and can occur after sigmoidoscopy with biopsy. M*yobacterium tuberculosis* is contracted by hematogenous contamination, although *Streptococcus viridans* is the most common organism.

Bowel Wall Entry. Infection contracted through the bowel wall is associated with an increased incidence of diverticular disease, severe vascular disease, and unresolved constipation. Enteric and anaerobic microorganisms are usually identified in this infection.

Infection is also known to occur through the female reproductive tract.

Host Defense Mechanisms

Particulate matter and bacteria are absorbed from the peritoneal cavity chiefly through the lymphatics. Peritoneal macrophages are the first line of cellular defense.

Responsible Organisms

Responsible organisms (National Institutes of Health, 1986) have been identified as follows:

- gram-positive, 55%
- gram-negative, 19%
- mixed gram-positive and gram-negative, 3%
- fungi, 3%
- other unusual organisms, less than 1%
- no growth, 17% (Inadequate culture techniques are believed to be responsible rather than sterile peritonitis.)
- no culture, 2.5%

The average peritonitis rate is 1.4 episodes per year (National Institutes of Health, 1986).

Patients at Risk

Patients at risk for peritonitis (National Institutes of Health, 1986) include

- patients younger than age 20 years
- patients older than age 60 years
- patients with diabetes mellitus
- patients with prior therapy for end-stage renal disease
- black patients, living with family

Signs and Symptoms

Turbidity of dialysate effluent (due to an increase in white blood cells and fibrin), abdominal discomfort or pain, and rebound tenderness are all symptoms of peritonitis. Less common signs and symptoms include fever, nausea, vomiting, and chills.

Clinical Course

The incubation period for touch contamination seems to be 24 to 48 hours, and the incubation period for endogenous infections is probably much shorter. Symptoms decrease dramatically after initiation of appropriate antibiotic therapy, and usually resolve within 2 or 3 days.

Differential Diagnosis

Differential diagnosis of peritonitis is made by a dialysate white blood cell count greater than $100/mm^3$, a dialysate white blood cell differential showing more than 50% neutrophils, and a positive culture.

Treatment

The treatment of choice for infection caused by gram-positive organisms is, for continuous dialysis, cephalosporin, 500 mg/L loading dose and 250 mg/2 L maintenance dose; for intermittent dialysis, cephalosporin, 50 to 100 mg/L.

The treatment of choice for infection caused by gram-negative organisms is, for continuous dialysis, tobramycin or gentamicin, 1.7 mg/kg of body weight intraperitoneal loading dose and 8 mg/L maintenance dose; for intermittent dialysis, tobramycin or gentamicin, 8 mg/L.

The treatment of choice for infection caused by mixed gram-positive and gram-negative organisms is, for both continuous dialysis and intermittent dialysis, a combination of the therapies for gram-positive and gram-negative organisms outlined.

Heparin, 500 U/L, is added to the dialysis solution because it will inhibit fibrin formation, which may prevent subsequent adhesion formation. The length of treatment is 10 to 14 days.

Fungal Peritonitis

Yeasts are the most common organisms in fungal peritonitis and can be seen on Gram stain. Fungi can colonize the Silastic catheter. The intraperitoneal administration of antifungal agents used to treat this form of peritonitis causes extreme irritation and pain. Early catheter removal and systemic chemotherapy are recommended to help reduce the increased morbidity and mortality seen in fungal peritonitis.

Mycobacterium Tuberculosis

The peritoneum is usually a secondary site for this infection, which is generally caused by hematogenous contamination. There is a positive history of tuberculosis, and the dialysate white blood cell differential shows a predominance of mononuclear cells. It is difficult to obtain a positive culture, although a peritoneal biopsy specimen may culture positive for tuberculosis.

Treatment consists of catheter removal and chemotherapy. Prophylactic antitubercular therapy should be considered in patients with positive tuberculin test, particularly transplant candidates.

Peritoneal Eosinophilia

Peritoneal eosinophilia is a noninfectious peritonitis that presents with a turbid dialysate and absence of abdominal pain or other symptoms of infection. The dialysate white blood cell count is relatively low. The white blood cell differential shows less than 50% neutrophils and more than 10% eosinophils. Peritoneal eosinophilia is thought to be an allergic response caused by a new peritoneal catheter or intraperitoneal medications. Treatment does not require antibiotic therapy; the condition resolves spontaneously.

Peritonitis that does not resolve can be traced to inappropriate or inadequate therapy, exit site or tunnel infection, ruptured viscera, intraperitoneal abscess, or colonization of the catheter.

Indications for catheter removal include

- unresolved peritonitis lasting more than 3 to 5 days
- tunnel infection
- fecal peritonitis
- fungal peritonitis
- tubercular peritonitis

Complications of peritonitis include

- abscess formation
- catheter loss
- transfer to hemodialysis therapy
- abdominal adhesions
- death

Exit Site Infection

Exit site infection is an inflammation of the catheter exit site with purulent drainage.

Responsible Organisms

Organisms that cause exit site infection include

- *Staphylococcus aureus*
- *Staphylococcus epidermidis*
- other gram-positive rods
- *Pseudomonas* species
- *Serratia* species
- other gram-negative organisms
- fungi

Risk Factors

Risk factors for exit site infection include

- failure to provide prophylactic antibiotic therapy at catheter insertion
- absence of dialysate leak or frank bleed
- cuff extrusion
- delayed or ineffective exit site healing
- upward-directed tunnel
- skin breakdown
- poor hygiene or poor exit site care
- trauma
- catheter manipulation (excessive torquing of the catheter; twisting of continuous ambulatory peritoneal dialysis extension tubing, or pulling on an unsecured catheter)
- sweating

Signs and Symptoms

Signs and symptoms of exit site infection include

- erythema
- induration
- tenderness or pain
- drainage (crust formation)

Diagnostic Criteria

The diagnosis of exit site infection can be made by the presence of erythema or induration with drainage, a drainage white blood cell differential that shows predominantly segmented cells, and a positive drainage culture.

Treatment

Treatment of exit site infection requires vigilant daily exit site care and assessment of response to cleansing agents. Topical antiseptics may be used in conjunction with antibiotic therapy, but topical antibiotic therapy is controversial. Antibiotic therapy may be given orally (cephalosporins, rifampin, trimethoprim/sulfamethoxazole, cloxacillin sodium; rifampin must be given in combination with one of the other antibiotics), intraperitoneally (cephalosporins, vancomycin hydrochloride, aminoglycosides), or intravenously (vancomycin).

Complications

Complications of exit site infection include

- tunnel infection
- peritonitis
- catheter removal
- transfer to hemodialysis

Subcutaneous Tunnel Infection

Risk Factors

Risk factors for subcutaneous tunnel infection include

- contamination during catheter insertion
- exit site infection
- delayed wound healing
- external cuff extrusion

Signs and Symptoms

Signs and symptoms of subcutaneous tunnel infection include

- irregularity; thickening along tunnel
- pain and tenderness along tunnel
- catheter loose in tunnel
- abscess over catheter tunnel
- large amount of purulent drainage from catheter exit site
- simultaneous peritonitis with same organism

Treatment

The treatments outlined for exit site infection may be attempted, but tunnel infections rarely, if ever, are cured. The catheter should be removed.

Complications

Complications of subcutaneous tunnel infection include

- abdominal wall cellulitis
- peritonitis
- transfer to hemodialysis

NONINFECTIOUS COMPLICATIONS OF PERITONEAL DIALYSIS

Surgical Complications Related to Catheter Insertion

Organ Perforation

Risk Factors.

- use of acute stylet catheter
- abdominal adhesions
- abdominal distention due to paralytic ileus, bowel obstruction, or constipation
- bladder distention

Signs and Symptoms.

- sudden abdominal pain
- massive watery diarrhea
- massive voiding of dialysate
- inadequate drainage of dialysate
- cloudy, odorous, or frankly fecal dialysate effluent

Diagnosis. Diagnosis is made by signs and symptoms and confirmed by a dipstick of urine or feces that is positive for glucose.

Intervention.

- bowel perforation
  1. monitor vital signs
  2. discontinue peritoneal dialysis
  3. remove catheter (perforation may seal spontaneously)
  4. administer antibiotic therapy
- bladder perforation
  1. monitor vital signs
  2. remove catheter
  3. drain bladder with Foley catheter
  4. reinsert peritoneal catheter
  5. monitor for peritonitis

Catheter Placed Preperitoneally

Risk Factor.

- use of acute stylet catheter

Assessment. If assessment reveals minimal or no drainage with initially clear drainage that becomes blood-tinged, the catheter should be removed.

Hemorrhage

Risk Factors.

- use of acute stylet catheter
- major vessel perforation

Signs and Symptoms.

- red or frankly bloody postoperative dialysate
- bleeding at catheter exit site
- shock

Assessment. Monitor drainage. Some blood-tinged dialysate after catheter insertion is normal; however, this usually resolves spontaneously during the first few exchanges. Bleeding that does not resolve and that intensifies, or dialysate that is grossly bloody, is abnormal.

Intervention.

- place ice packs or sandbags, and infiltrate epinephrine
- repair surgically
- replace fluid and blood losses

Complications Related to Peritoneal Catheter

Inability to Drain or Infuse

Cause.

- kinked or clamped tubing, external pressure on tubing
- kinked or bent catheter
- obstructed catheter (fibrin or blood clot)

Intervention.

- check entire length of tubing for kinks, pressure, and closed clamps
- check that catheter itself is not kinked or under external pressure
- obtain both abdominal flat plate and lateral view x-rays to confirm or rule out internal kinks
- use Fogarty embolectomy catheter or Italian corkscrew to attempt to remove clots from catheter (careful aseptic technique is mandatory)

One-Way Obstruction: Solution Can Be Infused but Will Not Drain

Cause.

- air lock in tubing interrupts siphon
- pressure on catheter from adjacent organs
- fibrin or blood clots surround terminal holes of catheter
- catheter placed incorrectly at insertion
- catheter has kink or bend
- catheter migration out of pelvis
- catheter wrapped in omentum
- fluid is loculated in an isolated area of the peritoneal cavity

Intervention.

- infuse small amount of additional dialysis solution (this will flush air bubbles out of the tubing); flush dialysis solution into the drain bag if Y tubing is used

- change body position
- induce peristalsis or a bowel movement if patient is constipated
- irrigate with a syringe containing heparinized dialysis solution (normal saline may flush fibrin or clots from the catheter and tubing) or move omentum away from the catheter
- obtain abdominal x-rays to confirm catheter malposition
- obtain both abdominal flat plate and lateral x-rays to confirm or rule out internal kinks
- obtain catheterogram using infusion of contrast media to identify loculus of fluid (has been associated with hypersensitivity reactions; contraindicated in patients who have a history of sensitivity to contrast medium)
- discontinue dialysis
- encourage ambulation and activity
- have patient assume knee-chest position
- attempt to reposition the catheter manually with a guidewire using aseptic procedure (often ineffective)
- reposition surgically or replace catheter
- perform omentectomy (rarely indicated)

Rectal or Suprapubic Pain

Cause.

- pressure from peritoneal catheter (more likely with acute stylet catheter)
- intraperitoneal catheter segment too long

Intervention.

- relieve pain and pressure with infusion of dialysis solution
- leave reservoir of fluid in peritoneal cavity between intermittent dialysis procedures to cushion the catheter

Catheter Cuff Extrusion

Cause.

- Silastic shape memory attempts to straighten the curved subcutaneous catheter segment and exerts a forward force on the external cuff

- tunnel is shorter than subcutaneous catheter segment
- external pulling and tugging on catheter
- placement of the external cuff too close to the skin

Assessment. Palpate the subcutaneous cuff (wear sterile gloves). If the cuff is visible at the skin surface the exit site is inflamed or infected.

Intervention.

- vigilant daily exit site care
- treat exit site infection
- shave off the cuff (reports do not show consistent results)
- remove catheter

Complications.

- chronic exit site infection
- subcutaneous tunnel infection
- peritonitis

Damage to Catheter

Cause and Risk Factors.

- accidental trauma
- shaved cuff
- use of inappropriate disinfectants
- barium-impregnated catheters
- defective catheter
- use of syringe and needle by untrained personnel to obtain dialysate sample
- use of toothed hemostat by untrained personnel to clamp catheter

Signs.

- wear line on catheter
- visible crack(s) in catheter
- distal segment stretching; loss of elasticity
- leakage of dialysate

Intervention.

- clamp catheter proximal to the site of damage
- disinfect immediately proximal to damaged area
- cut the catheter proximal to damaged area with sterile scissors
- resoak or scrub the open catheter with disinfectant for 5 minutes
- insert a new, sterile adapter
- administer prophylactic antibiotic therapy

Adapter Loose or Falls Out of Catheter

Cause.

- catheter stretching; loss of elasticity
- adapter used with catheter with too large an inner lumen (this is likely if catheter is relatively new)

Intervention.

- instruct the patient to clamp the catheter; cover the open catheter end with a povidone-iodine pad and sterile dressings; come to the emergency room immediately
- disinfect the catheter proximal to the stretched area with a 5-minute povidone soak and trim the catheter as outlined above
- disinfect the open catheter with a 5-minute povidone-iodine soak if catheter size is the problem and reinsert an appropriate-sized adapter

Intraperitoneal Loss of Acute Stylet Catheter

Risk Factors.

- inadequate anchoring during insertion
- dislodgment of sutures or shield by agitated or stuporous patient

Assessment. Catheter can be seen on x-ray and can be located by palpation.

Intervention.

- retrieve catheter surgically
- assess for peritonitis

Complications Related to Increased Intra-abdominal Pressure

Dialysate Leaks from Catheter Exit Site/Extravasation into Subcutaneous Tissues

- abdominal wall edema
- perineal edema
- penile edema

Cause.

- inadequate tissue ingrowth into catheter cuff due to immediate use after insertion, delayed healing, or poor insertion technique
- hernias
- trauma to catheter cuff
- tear or hole in catheter

Assessment. Document dialysis fluid balance. A blood glucose strip result will differentiate a dialysate leak from exit site exudate. Do a physical assessment.

Intervention—Acute Catheter.

- change dressings frequently using aseptic techniques
- protect skin with a barrier spray
- weigh patient frequently to estimate fluid loss accurately
- resuture exit
- replace peritoneal catheter

Intervention—Chronic Catheter.

- stop peritoneal dialysis for 14 days or longer to allow tissue ingrowth into cuff material
- secure the catheter and avoid its manipulation
- decrease exchange volume, dialyze in the supine position, and avoid activities that increase intra-abdominal pressure (coughing, Valsalva maneuver, straining, lifting) if peritoneal dialysis must be continued
- observe for development of peritonitis or catheter exit site or tunnel infection
- replace catheter if leak persists

Hernias

Cause.

- introduction of solution and increased intra-abdominal pressure may cause congenital or pre-existing hernias to become symptomatic
- increased intra-abdominal pressure during dialysis (especially continuous dialysis) may contribute to development of hernias

Location.

- inguinal
- incisional
- umbilical
- ventral

Assessment. Assess dialysate leakage (i.e., scrotal edema) related to inguinal hernia, and alleviate patient discomfort and disfigurement.

Intervention.

- repair the hernia
- delay peritoneal dialysis postoperatively or use low-volume exchanges and supine dialysis to minimize intra-abdominal pressure

Complications Related to Peritoneal Dialysis

Abdominal Pain

Cause.

- rapid inflow
- hypertonic solutions
- acidic pH of solutions

Intervention.

- slow infusion rate during initial exchanges
- avoid the use of hypertonic exchanges during early dialyses or alternate use of hypertonic exchanges in acute dialysis
- add sodium bicarbonate to the dialysis solution to raise the pH and alleviate symptoms

- add a local anesthetic to the dialysis solution
- change position of patient

Shoulder Pain

Cause.

- referred pain from the diaphragm
- abdominal distention
- air in the peritoneal cavity due to an infusion of air, accumulation of small amounts of air over time, or bowel perforation
- dialysate volume
- infusion pressure from malpositioned peritoneal catheter

Assessment. Evaluate patient complaints. Examine x-ray for presence of free air in the peritoneal cavity. Check chart for documented recent infusion of air. Assess patient for bowel perforation. Prevent air accumulation in intraperitoneal space by priming new tubings. Do not use vented systems. In manual systems, always close clamps at completion of solution infusion.

Intervention.

- initiate drainage with the patient in a knee-chest or Trendelenburg position after exchange using full exchange volume

Back Pain

Cause.

- neuromuscular diseases
- degenerative spinal disease or metabolic bone disease
- deconditioning due to abdominal muscle weakness, multiple abdominal surgeries, poor posture, poor exercise tolerance
- altered spinal mechanics in continuous peritoneal dialysis

Prevention and Intervention.

- identify high-risk patients
- teach good posture and proper body mechanics
- introduce muscle strengthening exercises
- use abdominal supports for patients with hernias or multiple scars

Outcome.

- transfer patients to intermittent form of peritoneal dialysis therapy if necessary

Fluid Overload

Cause.

- inadequate use of hypertonic solutions
- use of 1.5% dextrose solutions
- poorly functioning catheter
- dialysate leak
- inadequate sodium removal
- inaccurate calculations of fluid balance
- decreased insensible losses in chronic patients due to seasonal changes
- chronic subcutaneous dialysate leak
- excess intake
- increased salt and water intake in chronic dialysis patients
- inadequate or ineffective salt and water restrictions in acute patients

Assessment. Assess patient for positive fluid balance, blood pressure increase from baseline, weight gain, shortness of breath, peripheral edema, subcutaneous edema, neck vein distention, pulmonary edema, congestive heart failure, and tachycardia followed by bradycardia.

Intervention.

- use more hypertonic dialysis solution
- limit fluid intake
- calculate fluid balance accurately, including all losses and all sources of intake
- shorten dwell time
- correct catheter malfunction
- monitor vital signs frequently
- weigh patient frequently
- monitor cardiac and respiratory status

Fluid Deficit

Cause.

- excessive fluid removal
- excessive use of hypertonic solution
- excessive sodium removal
- inaccurate fluid balance calculations
- increased insensible loss in chronic patients due to seasonal changes
- inadequate intake
- decreased salt and water intake in chronic patients
- severe limitation in fluid and sodium intake in acute patients

Assessment. Evaluate patient for negative fluid balance, blood pressure decrease from baseline, weight loss from baseline (may be under anticipated dry weight), poor skin turgor, dry mucous membranes, and postural hypotension.

Tachycardia

Intervention.

- discontinue use of hypertonic solution
- replace fluid and sodium losses (bouillon or other salty liquid; intravenous replacement may be required in acute dialysis)
- calculate fluid balance accurately, including all sources of intake and all losses
- monitor vital signs and weight closely
- lengthen dwell time

Hypokalemia

Cause.

- excessive potassium removal in acute dialysis
- inadequate dietary intake in chronic dialysis

Assessment. Monitor serum chemistries. Ask patient about weakness, arrhythmias, and constipation.

Intervention.

- for acute dialysis patients use potassium-free dialysis solution only until potassium reaches normal limits
- add potassium chloride (2 to 4 mEq/L) to the dialysis solution for acute dialysis patients with normal serum potassium
- monitor serum potassium
- increase dietary intake for chronic peritoneal dialysis patients with low serum potassium
- if potassium supplementation is required for chronic dialysis patients, use oral supplements because they are less expensive and intraperitoneal potassium has inherent risk of contaminating the system

Blood-Tinged Dialysate

Cause.

- abdominal trauma
- menstruation
- ovulation
- abdominal disease

Assessment. Bleeding is minimal to moderate with this problem. The dialysate effluent will have diminishing color in subsequent exchanges. It may be prudent to rule out peritonitis and other acute abdominal disease.

Intervention.

- prevent clotting and maintain catheter patency by adding heparin to the dialysate
- bleeding will resolve

Acute Hydrothorax

Cause.

- structural defects in diaphragm, either congenital or acquired

Presentation.

- massive acute hydrothorax
- pleural effusion

- usually on right side
- usually discovered shortly after initiation of peritoneal dialysis

Assessment. With acute hydrothorax, the dialysate drains poorly. The patient has dyspnea, tachypnea, and decreased breath sounds. There is radiologic evidence of pleural effusion. The pleural fluid composition is similar to that of dialysate, with a high glucose and a high protein concentration. Add methylene blue to the dialysis solution to stain pleural fluid. Add radioactively tagged human albumin to the dialysis solution so that the isotope can be detected in the thorax.

Intervention.

- small effusions require monitoring only
- stop peritoneal dialysis if massive hydrothorax occurs
- CAPD patients are successfully transferred to IPD
- use talc and tetracycline for pleurodesis

Metabolic Complications of Chronic Peritoneal Dialysis

Amino Acid and Protein Losses

Assessment. Assess the patient for low serum albumin levels, low transferrin levels, and a decrease in total body nitrogen.

Intervention.

- increase dietary intake of protein
- increase amino acid absorption from dialysis solution
- check for increase in nitrogen and transferrin in dialysate

Glucose Absorption

Problems.

- increased total caloric load, if dietary intake is not modified
- prolonged increase in caloric load results in increased dry body weight

Intervention.

- monitor number of hypertonic exchanges, dietary patterns, serum triglycerides, and weight gain

- avoid simple carbohydrates in diet
- increase activity and exercise
- restrict alcohol consumption
- restrict fat intake
- administer insulin as ordered for diabetic patients; monitor serum glucose carefully

REFERENCES

National Institutes of Health. (1986). *Report of the national CAPD registry of the National Institutes of Health: Characteristics of participants and selected outcome measures for the period January 1–August 31, 1986.* Bethesda, MD: Author.

Twandowski, Z.J., Nolph, K.D., Khanna, R., Gluck, Z., Prowant, B.F., & Ryan, L.P. (1986). Daily clearances with continuous ambulatory peritoneal dialysis and nightly peritoneal dialysis. *ASAIO Transactions, 32,* 575–580.

SUGGESTED READINGS

Holloway, N.M. (1988). *Nursing the critically ill patient.* Menlo Park, CA: Addison-Wesley.

Prowant, B., & Binkley, L.S. (1987). Concepts and principles of peritoneal dialysis. In L.E. Lancaster (Ed.), *Core curriculum for nephrology nursing.* Pitman, NJ: American Nephrology Nurses' Association.

7
Transplantation

CRITERIA FOR TRANSPLANTATION

Age

Physiologic age rather than chronologic age is important in transplantation. Transplantation is the treatment of choice for renal failure in children; there is no lower age limit, but the limited availability of small organs creates a supply problem.

Etiology of Renal Disease

No specific renal disease categorically excludes a patient from receiving a kidney, with the exception of cancer of the kidneys, ureters, or bladder.

Patients with polycystic kidney disease may require bilateral nephrectomies to avoid post-transplantation complications, such as infection and bleeding from cysts, once the patient is immunosuppressed.

Patients with pyelonephritis may also require nephrectomies to prevent post-transplantation infection when immunosuppression has been achieved.

Patients with uncontrolled hypertension may require nephrectomies to control the production of renin.

Urinary Tract

The urinary tract must be free of infection. The prospective recipient must have a functional bladder and patent ureters (some centers accept patients requiring self-catheterization).

139

Cardiovascular System

The cardiovascular system must have adequate cardiac function, patent iliac vasculature, and minimal atherosclerotic disease.

Gastrointestinal System

The prospective recipient should not have peptic ulcer disease or intestinal diverticuli; if present, these disorders must be corrected prior to transplantation because steroids increase the risk of gastrointestinal bleeding and perforation. The recipient must have adequate hepatic function, since azathioprine and cyclosporine are hepatotoxic.

Pulmonary System

The pulmonary system must be evaluated for postoperative risk for pulmonary problems based on the immunosuppressed status of the patient. Chronic pulmonary disease may contraindicate transplantation because of the high risk of morbidity and mortality.

Endocrine System

Transplantation may be the treatment of choice for diabetics with end-stage renal disease, but these patients are at a greater risk for complications. Patients with hyperparathyroidism may require pretransplantation subtotal parathyroidectomy to prevent post-transplantation hypercalcemia.

Dental System

Teeth and gums should be in good condition before transplantation to prevent post-transplantation infection and hyperplasia related to cyclosporine administration.

Infection

The presence of an active infection is a contraindication to transplantation.

Psychosocial System

The patient must demonstrate adjustment to his or her illness. A careful family and social history should be obtained. Vocational and financial information also should be gathered. The patient should have an understanding of transplantation regimens and their implications (Weiskettle, Weems, Moran, Devney, & Chang, 1988). A history of psychiatric illness must be carefully evaluated, as post-transplantation steroid administration can aggravate an underlying psychiatric condition.

IMMUNOLOGIC BASIS OF TRANSPLANTATION
Introduction

The major function of the body's immune system is to defend the body against attack by foreign substances. In the case of transplantation, the body of the recipient perceives the newly transplanted kidney as a foreign substance and, unless altered, mounts an attack against the kidney.

Immunology in transplantation requires a match of donor and recipient kidneys, so that the recipient's body will defend against the new kidney as little as possible, and suppression of the recipient's defense (immune) system so that it is unable to adequately defend the body against the foreign organ.

ABO Compatibility

Donor and recipient must be compatible for the major blood groups (A, B, AB, and O).

Histocompatibility

Genetic Basis

Each ovum has 23 chromosomes. When they are joined at fertilization, 46 chromosomes (23 pairs) are present.

Genes are sites on chromosomes that carry the inheritance code for protein and enzyme synthesis. Genes determine the structure of antigens, which are protein molecules on the surfaces of cells that stimulate an immune response.

The antigens most readily identifiable on white blood cells are the most important in transplantation; they are called human leukocyte antigens (HLAs).

Expression of the HLAs is controlled by a single genetic region located on chromosome 6. Currently, HLAs can be identified that are coded at four regions (loci) on chromosome 6; these are the A, B, C, and D (or DR) regions.

The HLA region is inherited as a haplotype, that is, one of a pair of chromosomes from each parent (Figure 7-1).

Tissue Typing

HLA typing is done by lymphocytotoxicity testing performed on a venous blood sample. Lymphocytes are exposed to antisera with known antibodies; if the lymphocytes carry a cell surface antigen that is recognized by the antibodies, the lymphocytes are lysed, and the specific HLA antigen to which the antibody is reacting can then be identified.

White Blood Cell Crossmatch. A white blood cell crossmatch detects preformed antibodies in the recipient directed against the antigens expressed in donor cells. In a positive crossmatch, antibodies to the donor HLAs are present in the recipient serum; transplantation is contraindicated.

The presence of antibodies in serum varies over time, so specimens must be obtained on a regular basis and must be available for the final matching of donor and recipient.

Mixed Lymphocyte Culture. Mixed lymphocyte culture or mixed lymphocyte reaction determines the degree of D-locus compatibility between the donor and the recipient.

Modifying the Immune Response Pretransplantation

Pretransplantation Blood Transfusions. Multiple transfusions before cadaveric transplantation appear to improve graft survival in some cases; however, there are mixed reports regarding the efficacy of this regimen.

Donor-Specific Transfusion. In donor-specific transfusion, the recipient receives a blood transfusion from the potential donor; immune responsiveness is measured, and transplantation proceeds if the recipient does not develop antibodies. This procedure has been shown to improve graft survival, but it carries the risk of transmission of infections such as hepatitis, cytomegalovirus, and acquired immunodeficiency syndrome (all centers carefully screen for the viruses that cause these infections).

Splenectomy. Splenectomy is not advocated by all immunologists because it is a major surgical procedure. Splenectomy reduces lymphoid mass, thus decreasing lymphocyte production.

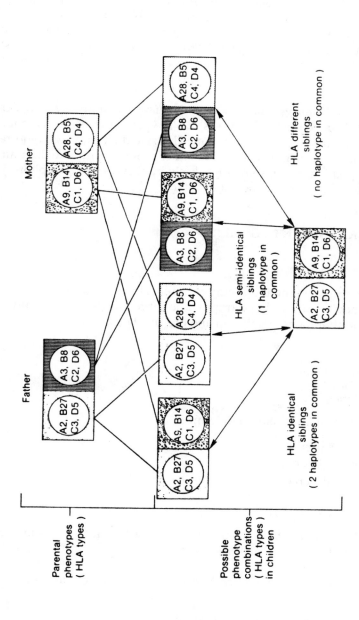

Figure 7-1 Mendelian inheritance of HLA antigens. *Source:* From *Clinical Immunology,* 2nd ed. (p. 457) by S.O. Freedman and P. Gold, 1976, New York: Harper and Row. Copyright 1976 by Harper and Row. Reprinted by permission of J.B. Lippincott.

Total Lymphoid Irradiation. Total lymphoid irradiation reduces lympho-cyte production. Low-dose irradiation of the thoracic-abdominal-lymphatic system is carried out for approximately 10 days; the leukocyte count must be monitored. This immunosuppressive method.is not advo-cated by many because of the potential for life-threatening infection post-transplantation. It is used primarily for second transplants or intractable rejection.

Thoracic Duct Drainage. Thoracic duct drainage currently is not widely used. For this procedure to be successful, the patient must be lymphoid depleted at the time of transplantation. Thoracic duct drainage requires placement of an indwelling catheter in either thoracic lymph duct, drain-ing the lymphatic system, removing the lymphocytes by hemaphoresis, and returning the lymph to the patient.

DONOR TRANSPLANT SURGERY

Match

Match for tissue typing is imperative; rarely is there a need to match for size, as a child's kidneys hypertrophy and large kidneys can usually be placed in the abdomens of children and of some large infants.

Living Related Donor

Initial Evaluation

The initial evaluation should determine

- histocompatibility
- willingness to donate
- initial health screening for obvious contraindications

Additional Evaluation

Further histocompatibility testing for the best match includes medical assessment and psychosocial assessment.

Medical Assessment. The medical assessment should include the follow-ing studies:

- complete history and physical examination
- chest x-ray

- electrocardiogram
- hematology, chemistry, and coagulation blood studies
- urine studies
- intravenous pyelogram, renal scan, renal arteriogram
- other studies as indicated

Psychosocial Assessment. The psychosocial assessment should determine

- the donor's understanding of nephrectomy and transplantation
- the donor's emotional reaction to donation
- the donor's concerns about the surgery
- the attitude of the donor's significant other about the donation
- the donor's psychosocial relationship with the potential transplant recipient
- vocational and financial information

Living Related Donor Nephrectomy

Nephrectomy is a major surgical procedure performed via a flank incision. Postoperative nursing care involves the performance of routine postoperative procedures to prevent pulmonary complications, as follows:

- maintain fluid balance
- monitor electrolytes
- prevent infections
- prevent/relieve pain (The donor often experiences more pain than the recipient because of the nephrectomy procedure and placement of the incision.)
- provide emotional support

Cadaveric Donor

Introduction

As of October 1987, all hospitals must have protocols for organ donation and procurement as a prerequisite to participation in the Medicare program. Routine inquiry or required request for organ donation by hospitals is legislated in more than half of the states in the United States.

General Criteria (May Vary by Institution)

The cadaveric donor must

- be younger than age 65 years
- have no history of malignancy
- have no history of renal disease or hypertension
- have no systemic infections
- have adequate renal function
- be brain dead (complete apnea despite levels of carbon dioxide sufficient to trigger respiration)
- demonstrate absence of all spontaneous movement
- demonstrate unresponsiveness
- demonstrate absence of all cephalic reflexes (spinal cord reflexes may continue to be present)
- have an electrocerebrally silent electroencephalogram

Donor Maintenance

The cadaveric donor's body functions must be maintained until consent can be obtained and the organs removed. Organ viability, blood pressure, and urine output must be maintained.

Consent from Next of Kin

Although witnessed organ donor cards are valid, most organ procurement agencies require consent from next of kin. The procedures must be carefully and compassionately explained to the family. Support must be provided regardless of the family's ultimate decision.

RECIPIENT TRANSPLANT SURGERY

Preoperative Nursing Care

Preoperative nursing care requires a complete physical assessment. Report abnormalities or contraindications to the transplant procedure to physicians and administer immunosuppressive medications and antibiotics as ordered. The patient may require dialysis.

Operative Placement of the Kidney

The kidney is usually placed in the anterior iliac fossa. This placement is advantageous because it precludes the need for an abdominal incision and facilitates anastomosis of the ureter and vessels and postoperative assessment of the kidney.

The renal artery is anastomosed end-to-end to the hypogastric artery or end-to-side to the external iliac artery.

The renal vein is attached end-to-side to the iliac vein.

The donor ureter is implanted in the recipient's bladder or attached to the stump of the recipient's ureter (Morris, 1984).

Postoperative Nursing Care

Maintaining Circulatory Function

Assess blood pressure, pulse, temperature, respirations, and central venous pressure every hour for the first 12 hours postoperatively, then every 4 hours.

Monitor the cardiac status for 24 to 48 hours post-transplantation.

Notify physicians of any signs or symptoms of cardiac distress, and take corrective action as indicated.

Maintaining Pulmonary Function

Deliver humidified oxygen at a concentration of 40% by face mask for 24 hours. Maintain pulmonary toilet.

Maintaining Fluid Balance

Common problems with attempting to maintain fluid balance include both fluid overload and dehydration. To minimize these problems, initially assess and record intake and output every 30 minutes or every hour for the first 12 hours, then every 4 hours thereafter.

Assess weight daily at the same time of day, on the same scale, with the patient wearing the same amount of clothing.

Measure and record vital signs and central venous pressure every 30 minutes or every hour for the first 12 hours, then every 4 hours thereafter.

Replace fluid in a volume of 1 mL for each milliliter of urine output, up to 250 mL/hour; if urine output is less than 50 mL/hour, notify physician.

Obtain blood specimens daily for blood urea nitrogen, creatinine, electrolytes, enzymes, and other studies; obtain a complete blood count and differential white blood cell count routinely.

Every 8 hours and as necessary, assess the patient for signs and symptoms of fluid imbalance: dry mucous membranes, decreased blood pressure, poor skin turgor, concentrated urine, shortness of breath, and peripheral edema.

Maintaining Electrolyte Balance

Common problems with attempting to maintain electrolyte balance include hyperkalemia and hyperglycemia. Monitor serum electrolytes and glucose daily.

Preventing Infections in Immunosuppressed Patients

Infection is the most common cause of mortality in the compromised host. Rapid isolation and identification of the etiologic agent are essential in ensuring the appropriate therapy and eradication of infection.

The following discussion explains the factors involved in infection and how they affect the immunosuppressed patient. The critical care nurse can play an important role in recognizing and preventing infection in the immunocompromised host.

FACTORS INVOLVED IN INFECTION

The Normal Host

Factors important to maintaining the well-being of the host are natural defenses, specific defenses, age, and nutritional status.

Natural Defenses

The host's natural defenses include physical barriers to entry by infectious agents, such as intact skin and mucosa; and chemical barriers, such as acid secretion by the gastric mucosa, and the acidity of urine, which offer a hostile environment.

A variety of lipids secreted by the skin provide other forms of protection. Physiologic mechanisms exist, as well, for emptying and cleansing hollow viscera. Mucus produced in the large airways of the lung, for example, traps inspired particles, which are then removed by the ciliary epithelium and expectorated. Still other defenses include the peristalsis in the gastrointestinal tract and the periodic emptying of the urinary bladder, which expel organisms from the internal environment of the host.

Specific Defenses

Specific defenses include phagocytotic cells, such as neutrophils, which provide a first line of defense against bacteria and certain fungi. Neutrophils kill organisms at the site of infection.

The immune system generates immune responses through the production of antibodies that circulate in the plasma (humoral immunity) or through the production of cells such as lymphocytes (cellular immunity).

The complement system is made up of a complex of proteins that are responsible for several steps in the inflammatory process, including directing phagocytotic cells to the site of infection. Complement also attaches to the infectious agent and promotes ingestion by the phagocyte.

The Immunosuppressed Patient

Immunosuppression is defined as the inability of the immune system to cope effectively with foreign antigens introduced into the body. There are two types of immunosuppression, congenital and acquired.

Congenital immunodeficiency disorders include a form known as combined immunodeficiency, a deficiency of lymphoid cells that mediate both cellular and antibody immunity. An individual born with this deficiency would be without a functional cellular or humoral immune system.

Acquired immunosuppression may occur during the course of many acute and chronic disease states.

The ability of patients in critical care units to prevent invasion by nosocomial pathogens is seriously compromised. Several conditions within the intensive care unit (ICU) are important determinants of infections.

The Environment

ICUs are centers for acutely ill patients who are often heavily colonized or infected with a variety of nosocomial pathogens.

ICUs are often designed as open bays without physical barriers. The spread of organisms is facilitated from patients who harbor large numbers of organisms when physical barriers are absent.

The probability of transmitting infection is compounded by crowding, which may be necessary to support the highly technical interventions.

Improper cleaning and care of equipment may contribute to infection.

The Infectious Agent

Both bacteria and fungi have been reported as causative agents in nosocomial infections. Nosocomial microbes exhibit several intrinsic properties that enable them to cause disease.

Virulence

Virulence is a measure of an organism's pathogenicity, or the frequency with which it produces observable clinical disease. Examples of virulent organisms are *Streptococcus pyogenes, Neisseria meningitidis,* and *Clostridium tetani.* Most organisms responsible for nosocomial infections in the ICU are not considered as virulent, but rather as opportunistic pathogens because the host is debilitated.

Adaptability

Several nosocomial pathogens are able to adapt to a variety of environmental extremes. *Acinetobacter, Pseudomonas aeruginosa,* and *Legionella pneumophila* can survive in environments with wide temperature fluctuations. This adaptability allows the organisms to establish reservoirs in the critical care environment.

Adherence

The first step in the process of infection is adherence of the microbe to host tissue. Properties of the infectious agent that facilitate adherence increase the likelihood that an organism will cause disease.

Colonial Protection

Some microbes, such as *P. aeruginosa,* produce an amorphous substance (biofilm) that protects the bacterial colony from hostile elements in the environment (Costerton, Lam, Lam, & Chan, 1983).

Toxin Production

Certain microbes produce several toxic substances that play an important role in the pathogenesis of nosocomial infections. *Staphylococcus aureus* produces several exotoxins, including leukocidin (which is cytotoxic for neutrophils), as well as enterotoxin F (the toxin responsible for toxic shock syndrome) (Arnow, Chou, Weil, Crass, & Bengoll, 1984) and exfoliatin, a toxin responsible for the scalded-skin syndrome (Piemont, Rasoamananjara, Fource, & Bruce, 1984).

The virulence factors of these exotoxins are not imperative for inducing disease. Enterococcus and *S. epidermidis* are among the most frequent pathogens responsible for nosocomial infections, yet they produce very little in terms of toxic substances (Zervos et al., 1987).

Antimicrobial Resistance

Bacteria have acquired several mechanisms for combating the toxic effects of antimicrobial agents. Some of these specific mechanisms include detoxification, altered transport across cell membranes, altered binding sites, and substitute metabolic pathways.

ETIOLOGY OF MICROBES IN THE CRITICAL CARE UNIT

Reservoirs

A reservoir is that site in the environment where the organism resides. An organism may reside in a human, animal, or plant, or it may be in inert material in the environment. The reservoir provides a source of nutrients and a niche conducive to replication and persistence. Reservoirs can be categorized as either exogenous or endogenous to the patient.

Exogenous Reservoirs

Environmental reservoirs in a critical care environment include water, air, and food, which is an uncommon reservoir for nosocomial pathogens. Molds and fungi, in particular *Aspergillus* sp., are among the few potential pathogens found in the air. High-efficiency air filters should make the air of little significance as a reservoir. Food can serve as a reservoir for nosocomial gram-negative bacteria. Environmental reservoirs are relatively unimportant sources of nosocomial pathogens in the ICU.

A second category of external reservoirs includes medical equipment, medications, antiseptics, and other patient care materials.

A third exogenous reservoir is the health care worker. The health care worker may carry and shed bacterial pathogens and transmit infectious agents when he or she is infected.

Endogenous Reservoirs

The most important reservoir for nosocomial pathogens in the critical care unit is the patient. Little can be done to eradicate nosocomial pathogens from endogenous reservoirs. Patients may be colonized with a variety of gram-positive, gram-negative, aerobic, and anaerobic bacteria.

Severity of underlying disease and frequent use of antibiotics alter normal flora that reside on the skin or in the upper airway and bowel. When normal antibiotic-susceptible flora are eradicated in the course of antibiotic therapy, patients may become colonized with large numbers of intrinsically resistant flora such as enterococcus, *S. epidermidis,* and *Candida* or with potential nosocomial pathogens such as resistant *Enterobacteriaceae* and *Pseudomonas* (Selden, Lee, & Wang, 1971). As these organisms increase in quantity and as the host becomes less able to defend against infection, the new flora invade the host and establish a nidus of infection.

ENVIRONMENTAL FACTORS THAT CHANGE THE ECOSYSTEM

Several conditions in the intensive care environment create pressures on the ecosystem that alter bacterial flora and infection rates. The use of antibiotics plays a role in altering endogenous microflora in individual patients.

Treating multiple patients with antibiotics in an ICU may result in the emergence of highly resistant strains of bacteria (Price & Sleigh, 1970).

The lengthy stay of patients in an ICU will also alter the ecosystem. Patients with long lengths of stay become reservoirs for highly resistant nosocomial pathogens (Selden, Lee, & Wang, 1971). These patients harbor the resistant pathogens in large quantity, especially when they are infected.

Inattention to hygiene by the health care staff may facilitate the spread of organisms from the patient reservoir to uninfected patients.

Introduction of new techniques or new equipment may also disturb the ecosystem by creating new, unsuspected reservoirs and by providing new modes of transmission.

INFECTIONS IN THE CRITICAL CARE UNIT

Pathogenesis of Infection

Colonization usually precedes infection following inoculation of a potential pathogen onto mucous membranes, such as in the upper airway or genitourinary tract. Colonization consists of replication and persistence of the organism on the mucosal surface or skin surface without invasion of host tissue.

Factors that create an imbalance in the patient's internal milieu and promote colonization with potential nosocomial pathogens include the severity of the underlying disease, the administration of antibiotics, and the insertion of foreign bodies.

After invasion of the host, microorganisms produce disease in several different ways. Some organisms are directly invasive, producing enzymes that digest and destroy host tissue. Invasion of the organism may occur locally (abscess), along tissue planes (cellulitis and fasciitis), or into the blood stream and from there throughout the body. Bacteria also produce disease by releasing toxins. Disease may result from the inflammatory response generated by the host against the invading pathogen.

Infection Sites

Nosocomial infections occur at many sites in patients admitted to ICUs.

Urinary Tract

The urinary tract is the most common site of nosocomial infections (Turck & Stamm, 1981). This is so despite the defense mechanisms that the urinary tract possesses, including immune and inflammatory defense mechanisms and nonspecific mechanisms of mechanical factors, mucosal, and ecologic defenses, and urine's inherent antimicrobial properties related to acidity and hyperosmolality.

Urinary tract defenses in ICU patients may be compromised by the urinary catheter, which defeats mechanical, mucosal, and voiding reflex defenses, and by the condom catheter, which allows stagnant urine to collect and support colonization of the urethral area (Kunin, 1984).

The production of alkaline urine and the loss of neurogenic bladder control may also predispose to infection.

Respiratory Tract

Defense Mechanisms. The upper respiratory tract has different types of mechanical protection against infection. The nasopharynx acts as a filter to screen out microorganisms, whereas the epiglottis and gag reflex mechanically prevent aspiration.

Mucosal and ecologic defense mechanisms of the upper respiratory tract usually prevent potentially pathogenic organisms from colonizing the tract by decreasing the mucosal adherence of bacteria and providing an environment populated by bacteria that limit the growth of pathogenic microorganisms.

The lower airways are protected by both mechanical clearance and immune defenses.

The alveoli are protected primarily by the immune and inflammatory systems. Alveolar macrophages phagocytose and then process antigen, which is then carried to local lymphatics, where intracellular interaction between T and B lymphocytes in the presence of antigen promotes the production of sensitized T cells, killer lymphocytes, and effector B cells. Sensitized T cells migrate through the lymphatics, enter the general circulation, and return to the lung. When re-exposed to antigen, these cells release lymphotoxins and lymphokines, such as migration inhibition factor and macrophage activation factor. The lymphokines activate alveolar macrophages and enhance their ability to kill microorganisms. Killer lymphocytes are important in controlling cells infected by virus. Effector B cells differentiate into plasma cells, which secrete various classes of circulating immunoglobulins. After these immunoglobulins bind to an antigen, the inflammatory system is activated, initiating the complement cascade that releases chemotactic factors that attract neutrophils and other phagocytotic cells (Green, Jakob, Low, & David, 1977; Kaltreider, 1976).

Infectious Complications. Compromises of the aforementioned defense mechanisms may lead to different infectious complications. ICU patients are often obtunded or intubated, which may depress the gag reflex and predispose to microaspiration of oropharyngeal contents. The bacterial flora of the oropharynx often changes within 24 hours of hospitalization as a result of increased adherence of microorganisms to epithelial cells and a decrease in the number of nonpathogenic bacteria.

Other mechanical defenses of the respiratory tract that may be compromised in ICU patients are suppression of the cough reflex by narcotics and depression of mucociliary clearance by high inspired oxygen clearance (Sackner, Landa, Hirsch, & Zapata, 1975).

The Integument

Compromises of the integument are common in critical care patients. Wound infections may be the result of surgical or traumatic loss of skin barrier integrity. Some disruptions of the integument are intentional, such as in ventriculostomies and placement of orthopedic pins, surgical drains, intravascular catheters, temporary pacemakers, and other appliances. Both inflammation and immune mechanisms of the integument can be compromised by malnutrition and medications.

The Blood Stream

Bacteria may be introduced into the blood stream by disruptions in the barrier defenses of the skin. Normal hosts can adequately defend against transient bacteremia through immune and inflammatory mechanisms. Tissue macrophages in organs such as spleen, liver, and lungs also serve to defend against bacteremia by acting as physiologic filters to clear microorganisms from the blood stream.

Mechanisms for clearing bacteria from the blood stream frequently are compromised in the ICU. Intravascular devices provide a continual source for the introduction of microorganisms into the blood stream.

The Central Nervous System

Infection of the central nervous system is a major medical problem, especially in the immunocompromised patient. In compromised individuals, infection is caused by a much larger variety of organisms than those found in the general population. Clinical signs and symptoms may be subtle or absent owing to a lack of an inflammatory response.

Nursing Assessment of Immunocompromised Patients in the Critical Care Unit

Frequent nursing assessment of immunocompromised patients is critical. During assessment, the critical care nurse should be extremely attentive to possible sites of infection. This includes assessing for any signs of local inflammation or systemic infection and for changes in temperature and laboratory data, particularly the white blood cell count and differential count. Patients with neutropenia make recognition of infection difficult. Fever may be the only sign of infection in these patients.

Close observation should be given to intravenous catheter sites and pressure points for any signs of impending infection.

Auscultation for adventitious sounds in the lung fields should be performed frequently.

Infection monitoring in the ICU includes obtaining specimens from patients for culture for pathogenic organisms and examining patients for physiologic, hematologic, and biochemical abnormalities that may indicate infection.

Prevention of Nosocomial Infections in the Critical Care Unit

Various measures should be taken by the nurse in the ICU to prevent infection, especially in the immunocompromised patient.

Frequent and thorough handwashing is imperative. Strict aseptic technique in the care of all possible sites of entry of infection is vital. These sites include all catheters, central lines, endotracheal tubes, pressure monitoring lines, and peripheral intravenous lines.

Special precautions that should be taken in the care of the immunosuppressed patient include the following:

- frequent and thorough washing of hands before, during, and after patient care
- use of private rooms with door closed to avoid infection transmission (this may not be possible in all ICUs)
- use of masks by all persons with infections of the upper respiratory tract who must enter the patient's room
- use of masks for both patient and nurse when a central line is entered

Skin care is very important in the immunosuppressed patient. The ICU nurse should assess all pressure areas closely for signs of infection or breakdown. The skin should be well lubricated, since dry skin can crack and allow breakdown to begin.

Pulmonary toilet should be performed every 2 to 4 hours. Many of the opportunistic organisms lead to pneumonia. Frequent pulmonary assessments and coughing, deep breathing, and postural drainage are critical for prophylaxis and early detection of infection.

Adequate nutrition of the immunosuppressed patient is very important. For this patient to redevelop the immune system, he or she must have a high-protein, high-calorie diet. The effectiveness of all nutritional therapy should be evaluated weekly by a dietitian.

Provision and Monitoring of Immunosuppression

The primary purpose of immunosuppression is to block the body's response to foreign antigens. The major concerns in any immunosuppressive regimen are compromise of the patient's immunoresponsiveness and the adverse effects associated with each of the medications used. Some of the immunosuppressive medications currently in use are outlined below, along with adverse effects and nursing implications.

Prednisone/Methylprednisolone

Prednisone/methylprednisolone is an anti-inflammatory corticosteroid that acts by interfering with T cell differentiation and macrophage function, thereby impairing antigen recognition and cytotoxic response.

Corticosteroids were among the first immunosuppressive agents used and remain an important part of immunosuppressive therapy today.

Peak blood concentration is reached in 1 to 2 hours; biologic effects persist for 12 to 24 hours.

Adverse Effects.

- increased susceptibility to infection
- cushingoid appearance (moon face)
- hypertension
- peripheral edema
- gastrointestinal muscosal ulceration
- aseptic bone necrosis
- alterations in glucose metabolism (steroid-induced diabetes)
- muscle weakness
- hirsutism
- mood swings (euphoria to depression)

- cataracts
- pancreatitis

Because significant side effects can occur with long-term use, the lowest possible dosages are prescribed.

Nursing Implications.

- administer antacids as ordered to prevent gastric ulceration
- monitor blood glucose levels for changes in glucose metabolism
- minimize muscle weakness by early and frequent ambulation and leg exercises

Azathioprine

Azathioprine (Imuran) is an antimetabolite derivative of 6-mercaptopurine that interferes with nucleic acid synthesis; it prevents rapid growth of lymphocytes.

Adverse Effects.

- bone marrow toxicity (leukopenia and thrombocytopenia)
- myelotoxicity
- hepatotoxicity
- alopecia

Nursing Implications.

- monitor white blood cell and platelet counts for depression secondary to drug therapy
- monitor liver function studies for signs of hepatotoxicity

Cyclophosphamide

Cyclophosphamide (Cytoxan) is an antimetabolite derivative of 6-mercaptopurine; it is less toxic than azathioprine, but also less effective. It is used instead of azathioprine in patients who experience hepatotoxicity. Adverse effects and nursing implications are similar to those of azathioprine.

Cyclosporine

Cyclosporine (Sandimmune) is a metabolite of a strain of *Fungi Imperfecti* that interferes with the production, release, and action of interleukin-II, which is necessary for the growth and activation of T lymphocytes.

Adverse Effects.

- nephrotoxicity (generally dose-related and reversible)
- hypertension
- hepatotoxicity
- seizures
- hirsutism
- tremors
- gingival hyperplasia

Nursing Implications.

- monitor cyclosporine through levels as ordered

The oral solution is based in olive oil and is considered unpalatable by most patients. It is usually given in chocolate milk or orange juice. The oral solution should not be given in Styrofoam or paper receptacles because of its adherence to those materials.

The intravenous dosage is only one third the oral dosage; it should be administered diluted in 5% dextrose (in water) or normal saline in at least a 1:10 concentration; it should be given by a slow intravenous infusion over at least 3 to 4 hours.

Antithymocyte Globulin

Antithymocyte globulin is a preparation of antibodies to human T lymphocytes produced in sensitized animals. It is thought to diminish the number of functional or circulating T cells (i.e., thymocytes and lymphocytes).

Adverse Effects.

- anaphylactic reaction
- fever
- chills
- serum sickness
- malaise
- thrombocytopenia
- leukopenia

- arthralgia
- myalgia

Nursing Implications.

- administer always through a central venous line to prevent sclerosis of peripheral veins (intravenous administration usually takes 4 to 6 hours)
- administer premedications (usually diphenhydramine, acetaminophen, methylprednisolone) as ordered to minimize side effects
- monitor white blood cell and platelet counts for depression secondary to drug therapy

Orthoclone OKT$_3$

Orthoclone OKT$_3$ (Muromonab CD3) is a monoclonal antibody to the T$_3$ antigen of human T cells; it reverses graft rejection by blocking T cell function.

Adverse Effects.

- high fever (104° to 105° F)
- chills
- respiratory distress
- nausea, vomiting
- diarrhea
- headache

Nursing Implications. Prior to receiving the first dose, the patient needs to be free of any fluid overload as evidenced by a clear chest x-ray within 24 hours of treatment and have less than a 3% weight gain in the last 7 days.

- assess breath sounds and look for signs of peripheral edema
- administer premedications (usually diphenhydramine, acetaminophen, methylprednisolone) as ordered to minimize side effects
- give hydrocortisone (100 mg) intravenously 30 minutes after the first dose of OKT$_3$ to minimize potential respiratory effects
- assess the patient frequently during and after the first dose of OKT$_3$ to detect any respiratory difficulties
- provide cooling mattress if fever persists
- assess the patient carefully for signs of infection (Moir, 1989)

Observation and Treatment of Complications

Rejection

Hyperacute Rejection. Hyperacute rejection is associated with the presence of preformed antibodies to donor antigens at the time of transplantation. Graft function ceases within 24 hours, with the kidney becoming swollen and tender. Hyperacute rejection is accompanied by fever, leukocytosis, and thrombocytopenia. Reversal is rare.

Acute Rejection. Acute rejection most often occurs within the first 3 months after transplantation. Acute rejection usually indicates immunologic sensitization; it is predominantly a cell-mediated reaction and is accompanied by decreased urine volume and mild hypertension. Cyclosporine toxicity must be ruled out before a diagnosis of acute rejection is made. Acute rejection is generally treated with steroids or monoclonal antibodies.

Chronic Rejection. Chronic rejection usually does not occur earlier than 6 months post-transplantation. It results in progressive deterioration of graft function accompanied by hypertension and mild proteinuria.

Management of Rejection

Assess for clinical signs and symptoms of rejection every 8 hours and as necessary. Signs and symptoms of rejection include the following: temperature greater than 100° F; rapid weight gain (exceeding 3 lb/day); swollen and tender graft; decreased urine output; edema of eyelids, hands, or feet; pain on urination; bloody or odorous urine; increased blood pressure, with diastolic pressure greater than 100 mm Hg; shortness of breath. For any of these signs or symptoms administer additional immunosuppressive therapies as ordered.

Renal Artery Thrombosis. The incidence of renal artery thrombosis is low. Early detection is required for treatment to be effective. Anuria is the most obvious symptom of renal artery thrombosis. Treatment is immediate surgical repair.

Renal Artery Stenosis. Renal artery stenosis results in hypoperfusion of the kidney, which then produces more renin to compensate, causing hypertension. A bruit over the graft site is diagnostic evidence that can be confirmed by arteriography. Treatment includes antihypertensive medication; surgery is often needed.

Renal Vein Thrombosis. Renal vein thrombosis occurs rarely. Signs and symptoms include swelling of the graft as well as the affected thigh and leg, decreased urine output, and proteinuria. Renal vein thrombosis is treated with anticoagulation therapy.

Graft Rupture. Graft rupture is usually caused by swelling of the graft during a rejection episode. Surgery is almost always required. A swollen, painful graft site should warn of possible rupture and bleeding.

Urologic Complications. Urine leaks represent a urologic complication that results from ureteral leakage, ureteral disruption, or a leak from the bladder. The presence of urine leaks is related primarily to poor tissue healing or poor vascularity with tissue necrosis. Signs and symptoms of urine leaks include decreased urine output and edema and pain at the graft site.
Ureteral obstruction is indicated by decreased urine output, hematuria, and pain at the graft site.

Wound Complications. Wound complications include perinephric hematomas, urinomas, lymphoceles, and abscesses that can exert pressure on the kidney or ureter. They can result in deterioration of renal function and can also serve as a medium for infection. Signs and symptoms are a swollen, tender transplant site; fever; and wound drainage.

Other Postoperative Nursing Care

Administer pain medications as required in the immediate postoperative period. The patient may require post-transplant dialysis if rejection, cyclosporine nephrotoxicity, or acute renal failure occurs.

REFERENCES

Arnow, P.M., Chou, T., Weil, D., Crass, B.A., & Bengoll, M.S. (1984). Spread of a toxic-shock syndrome associated strain of *Staphylococcus aureus* and management of antibodies to staphylococcal enterotoxin F. *Journal of Infectious Disease, 149,* 103–107.

Costerton, J.W., Lam, J., Lam, K., & Chan, R. (1983). The role of the microcolony mode of growth in the pathogenesis of *Pseudomonas aeruginosa* infections. *Review of Infectious Disease, 5,* 5867–5873.

Green, G.M., Jakob, G.J., Low, R.B., & David, G.S. (1977). Defense mechanisms of the respiratory membrane. *American Review of Respiratory Disease, 115,* 479–514.

Kaltreider, H.B. (1976). Expression of immune mechanisms of the respiratory membrane. *American Review of Respiratory Disease, 113,* 347–349.

Kunin, C.M. (1984). Genitourinary infections in the patient at risk: Extrinsic risk factors. *American Journal of Medicine, 76*(5A), 131–139.

Moir, E.J. (1989). Nursing care of patients receiving orthoclone OKT$_3$. *ANNA Journal, 16*(5), 327–328, 366.

Morris, P.J. (1984). *Kidney transplantation: Principles and practice* (2nd ed.). New York: Grune & Stratton.

Piemont, Y., Rasoamananjara, D., Fource, J.M., & Bruce, T. (1984). Epidemiological investigation of exfoliative toxin-producing *Staphylococcus aureus* strains in hospitalized patients. *Journal of Clinical Microbiology, 19,* 417–420.

Price, D., & Sleigh, J. (1970). Control of infection due to *Klebsiella* in a neurosurgical unit by withdrawal of antibiotics. *Lancet, 2,* 1213–1215.

Sackner, M.A., Landa, J., Hirsch, T., & Zapata, A. (1975). Pulmonary effects of oxygen breathing: A 6-hour study in normal man. *Annals of Internal Medicine, 82,* 40–43.

Selden, R., Lee, S., & Wang, W.L. (1971). Nosocomial *Klebsiella* infections: Intestinal colonization as a reservoir. *Annals of Internal Medicine, 74,* 657–664.

Turck, M., & Stamm, W. (1981). Nosocomial infection of the urinary tract. *American Journal of Medicine, 70,* 651–654.

Weiskettle, P., Weems, J., Moran, S., Devney, P., & Chang, A. (1988). *Living with renal transplantation.* East Hanover, NJ: Sandoz Pharmaceuticals.

Zervos, M.J., Kauffman, C.A., Therasse, P.M., Bergman, A.G., Mikesell, T.S., & Schaberg, D.S. (1987). Nosocomial infection by gentamicin-resistant *Streptococcus faecalis. Annals of Internal Medicine, 106,* 687–691.

SUGGESTED READING

Schoengrund, L., & Balzer, P. (1985). *Renal problems in critical care.* New York: Wiley.

Ulrich, B.T., & Irwin, B.C. (1987). *Core curriculum for nephrology nursing.* Pitman, NJ: American Nephrology Nurses' Association.

Index

DATE DUE

NOV 1 4 1993		
NOV 2 2 1994		
MAR 2 2 1995		
MAR 0 2 1995		
NOV 1 6 2000		
NOV 2 1 2000		
APR 0 1 2003		

DEMCO 38-297